...BEFORE THE

DARK TIMES...

MYSTERIES OF THE JEDI

WRITTEN BY
ELIZABETH DOWSETT
AND SHARI LAST

CONTENTS

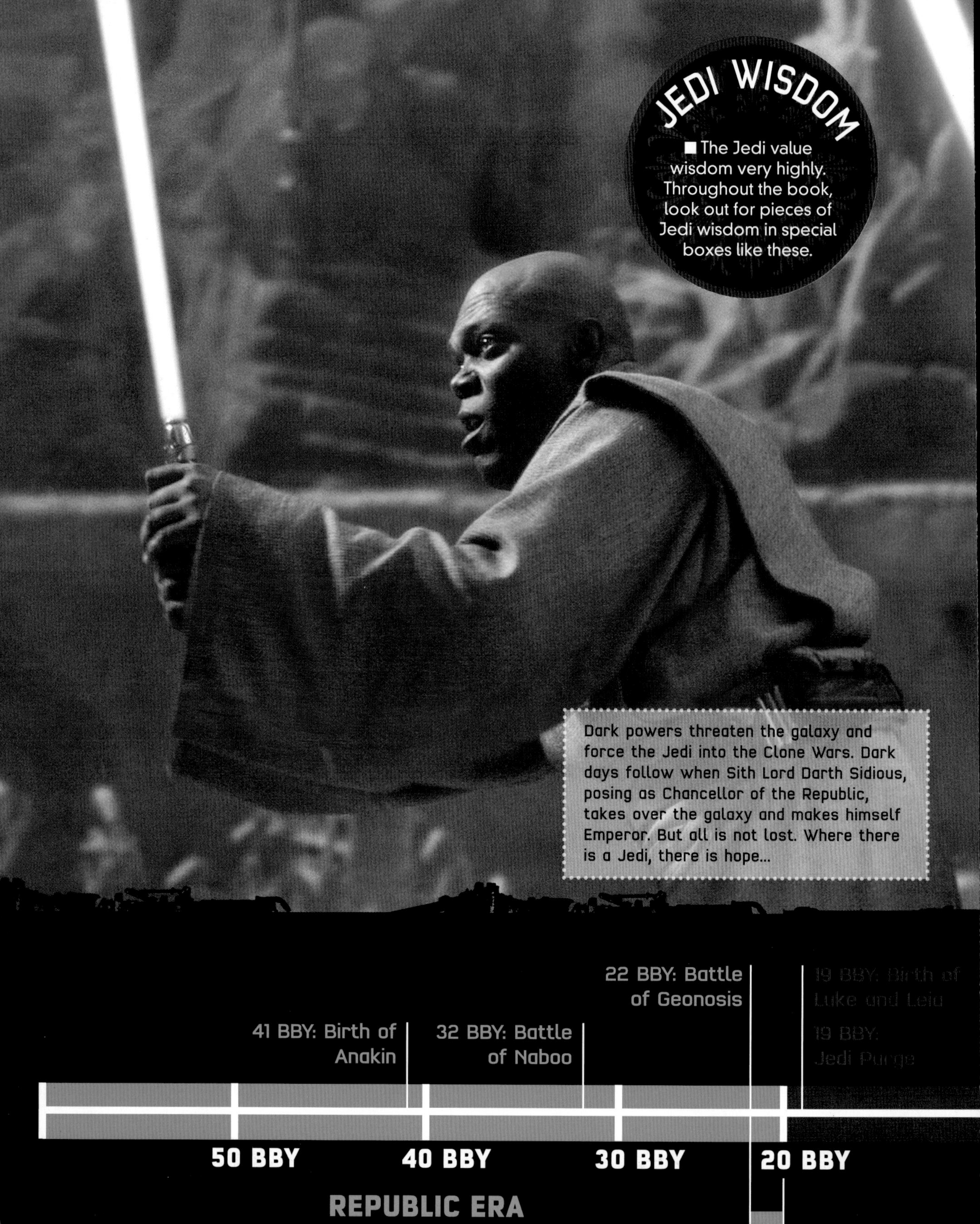

JEDI WISDOM

■ The Jedi value wisdom very highly. Throughout the book, look out for pieces of Jedi wisdom in special boxes like these.

Dark powers threaten the galaxy and force the Jedi into the Clone Wars. Dark days follow when Sith Lord Darth Sidious, posing as Chancellor of the Republic, takes over the galaxy and makes himself Emperor. But all is not lost. Where there is a Jedi, there is hope...

THE JEDI

The word Jedi is known throughout the galaxy. It carries respect and wonder. Mention of the Jedi conjures up images of noble defenders of peace and justice, selfless heroes who put the Republic before themselves.

Despite the popularity of the Jedi, however, little is actually known about the inner workings of this ancient Order. Who exactly are these powerful knights? How do they use a kind of mystical energy known as the Force? How do you become a Jedi and what is it like to dedicate your life to a higher purpose? Welcome to the mysteries of the Jedi...

NOTE ON DATES: Dates are fixed around the Battle of Yavin in year 0. All events prior to this are measured in terms of years Before the Battle of Yavin (BBY). Events after it are measured in terms of years After the Battle of Yavin (ABY).

0 Battle of Yavin

3 ABY: Battle of Hoth

2 BBY: Rebel Alliance is founded

4 ABY: Battle of Endor

10 BBY 0 10 ABY 20 ABY

THE FORCE HAS TWO SIDES

THE FORCE IS AN invisible energy that flows through all living things. Studying the Force will grant you knowledge and power. You must use this power wisely, or face the consequences.

THE LIGHT SIDE

The Jedi study the light side of the Force and use their wisdom to uphold justice and protect the innocent. Using the Force allows Jedi to live in harmony with the galaxy, feel things before they see them, react quickly to danger, and use a lightsaber with incredible skill.

- BRAVERY
- WISDOM
- LOYALTY
- INNER STRENGTH
- JUSTICE

PASSION ■

FORBIDDEN KNOWLEDGE ■

FREEDOM ■

GREAT STRENGTH ■

RAW POWER ■

THE DARK SIDE

The Sith study the dark side of the Force, which feeds on negative feelings such as anger, fear, and jealousy. The dark side offers almost unlimited power and access to dangerous knowledge, but at a terrible price. Submitting to the dark side transforms the Sith into something so evil, they cease to be human.

WHICH WOULD YOU CHOOSE?

FORCE JUMP

CHANNEL THROUGH: Full body
BEST FOR: Leaping out of harm's way; quick movement during a duel; surprising enemies from a great height.
LEARN FROM: Yoda, who evades his enemies during a duel with multiple Force jumps.
DANGER LEVEL: Moderate

USING THE FORCE

The Force might be invisible, but it can be channeled through a Jedi's body for a range of different results.

FORCE DEFLECTION

CHANNEL THROUGH: Hands
BEST FOR: Shielding yourself from incoming attacks.
LEARN FROM: Yoda, who repulses deadly Sith lightning fired at him by Chancellor Palpatine.
DANGER LEVEL: High

FORCE PILOTING

CHANNEL THROUGH: Hands and eyes
BEST FOR: Steering through busy airways.
LEARN FROM: Anakin, who flies safely at super speed above Coruscant.
DANGER LEVEL: High

FEEL THE FORCE

THE FORCE IS AN ENERGY FIELD that flows through every living thing and is accessible to those with the right mindset and training. Jedi spend many years studying how to apply its many uses without causing harm to themselves or others. Do you seek advice? Are you being attacked? The Force can help.

TELEKINESIS

CHANNEL THROUGH: Hands
BEST FOR: Moving objects without touching them; summoning your lightsaber.
LEARN FROM: Yoda, who uses the Force to stop heavy objects from crushing himself and others during his battle with Count Dooku.
DANGER LEVEL: Moderate

BEAST CONTROL

CHANNEL THROUGH: Hands and mind
BEST FOR: Taming wild beasts that threaten your safety.
LEARN FROM: Anakin, who takes control of a particularly vicious reek in the execution arena on Geonosis.
DANGER LEVEL: High

FORCE GHOST

CHANNEL THROUGH: Spirit
BEST FOR: Living on after death to advise and guide others.
LEARN FROM: Obi-Wan, who becomes one with the Force after sacrificing himself on the Death Star.
DANGER LEVEL: Low, but only possible for a few rare Jedi.

FORCE DISTURBANCE

CHANNEL THROUGH: Heart and mind
BEST FOR: Sensing disturbances in the Force; letting you know what is happening elsewhere in the galaxy.
LEARN FROM: Yoda, who senses the start of the Jedi Purge.
DANGER LEVEL: Low

SITH COMBAT

The Sith uses the dark side of the Force to fight viciously. Force choking weakens or kills through strangulation. Count Dooku uses it to attack Obi-Wan Kenobi. Force lightning is deadly blue crackling energy. These cruel uses of the Force are forbidden for Jedi.

JEDI MIND TRICK

CHANNEL THROUGH: Hands and mind
BEST FOR: Persuading others to leave you alone or to do what you want.
LEARN FROM: Obi-Wan, who convinces a stormtrooper patrol to let him pass through a checkpoint at Mos Eisley.
DANGER LEVEL: Low, but mind tricks work only on the weak-minded. A Jedi must be very careful not to abuse this power.

SMALL BUT STRONG

Never underestimate Yoda! Being small doesn't mean he can't be deadly. Yoda's strength comes from the Force. He achieves any height he needs in battle thanks to acrobatic Force jumps. When Count Dooku realizes that Yoda is more than a match for him, he flees in his Solar Sailer.

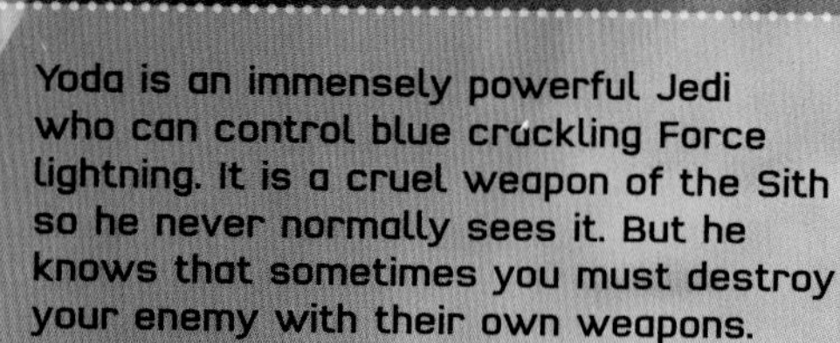

Yoda is an immensely powerful Jedi who can control blue crackling Force lightning. It is a cruel weapon of the Sith so he never normally sees it. But he knows that sometimes you must destroy your enemy with their own weapons.

YODA

Yoda is Grand Master of the Jedi Council. He shoulders the great responsibility of leading the Jedi Order. Famous for his unmatched wisdom, Yoda has a strong connection with the Force and often turns to it for answers.

JEDI STATS

SPECIES: UNKNOWN

HOMEWORLD: CORUSCANT

BIRTHDATE: 896 BBY

HEIGHT: 66 CM (2 FT 2 IN)

RANK: JEDI GRAND MASTER

TRAINED BY: UNKNOWN

WEAPON: GREEN-BLADED LIGHTSABER

PREFERRED COMBAT STYLE: FORM IV (ATARU)

TRADEMARK: WISDOM

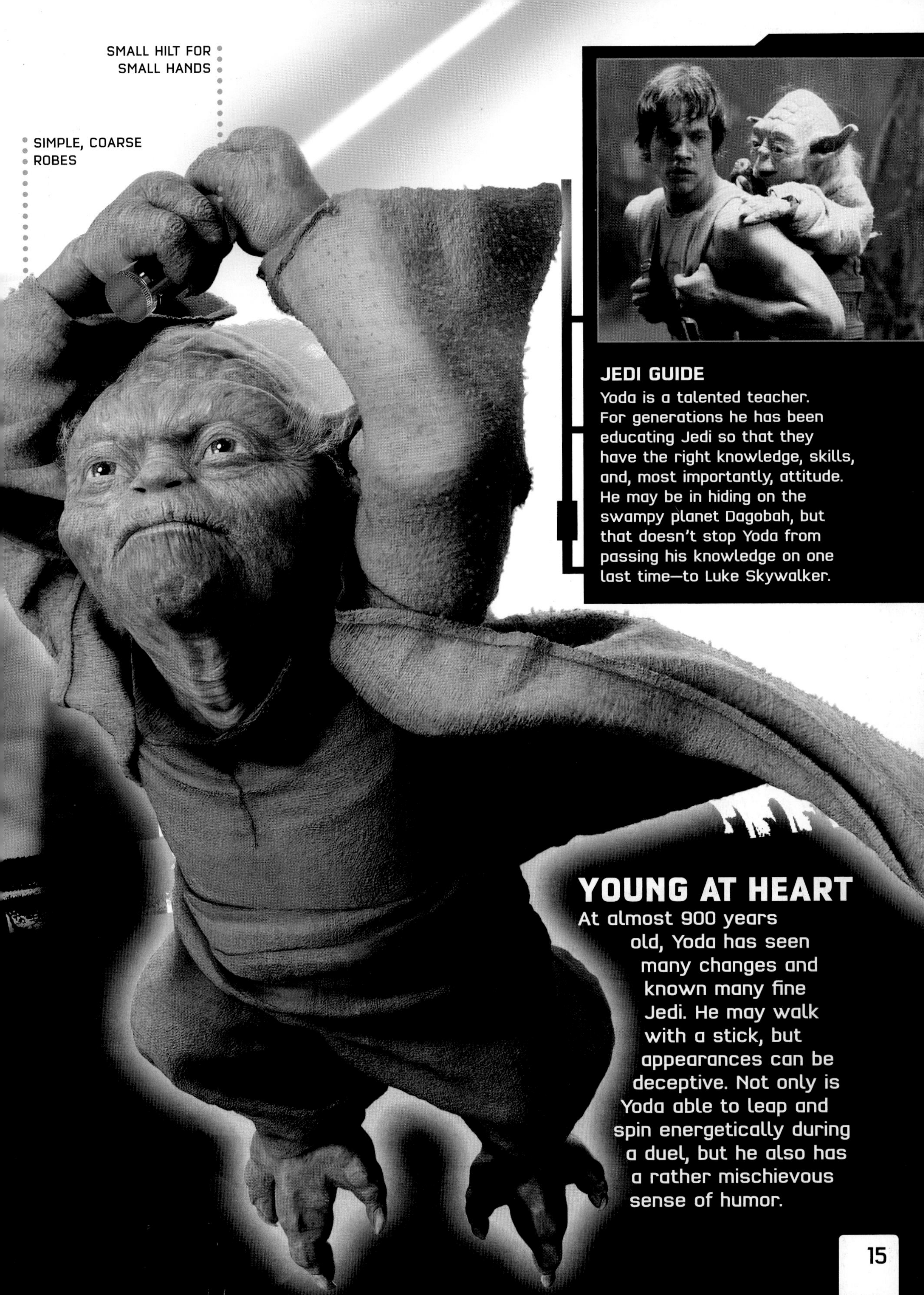

JEDI GUIDE

Yoda is a talented teacher. For generations he has been educating Jedi so that they have the right knowledge, skills, and, most importantly, attitude. He may be in hiding on the swampy planet Dagobah, but that doesn't stop Yoda from passing his knowledge on one last time—to Luke Skywalker.

YOUNG AT HEART

At almost 900 years old, Yoda has seen many changes and known many fine Jedi. He may walk with a stick, but appearances can be deceptive. Not only is Yoda able to leap and spin energetically during a duel, but he also has a rather mischievous sense of humor.

HOW DOES YODA FIGHT SOMEONE SO MUCH BIGGER THAN HIM?

YODA KNOWS THAT size matters not. The aged Jedi Grand Master is a skilled lightsaber warrior who can leap high and fight hard. When he takes on Darth Sidious in the Senate building on Coruscant, Yoda proves that his strength and power have nothing to do with his size.

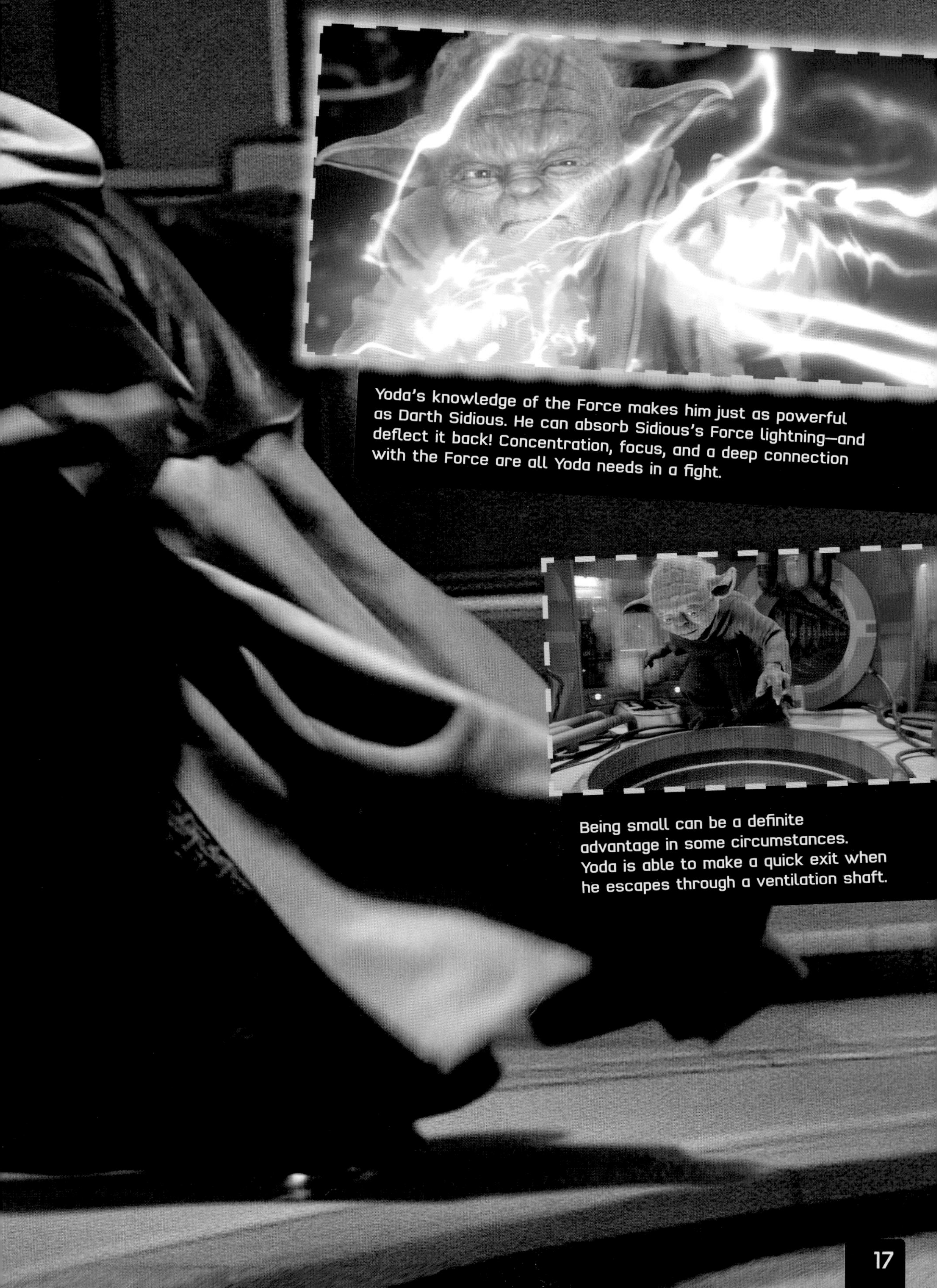

Yoda's knowledge of the Force makes him just as powerful as Darth Sidious. He can absorb Sidious's Force lightning—and deflect it back! Concentration, focus, and a deep connection with the Force are all Yoda needs in a fight.

Being small can be a definite advantage in some circumstances. Yoda is able to make a quick exit when he escapes through a ventilation shaft.

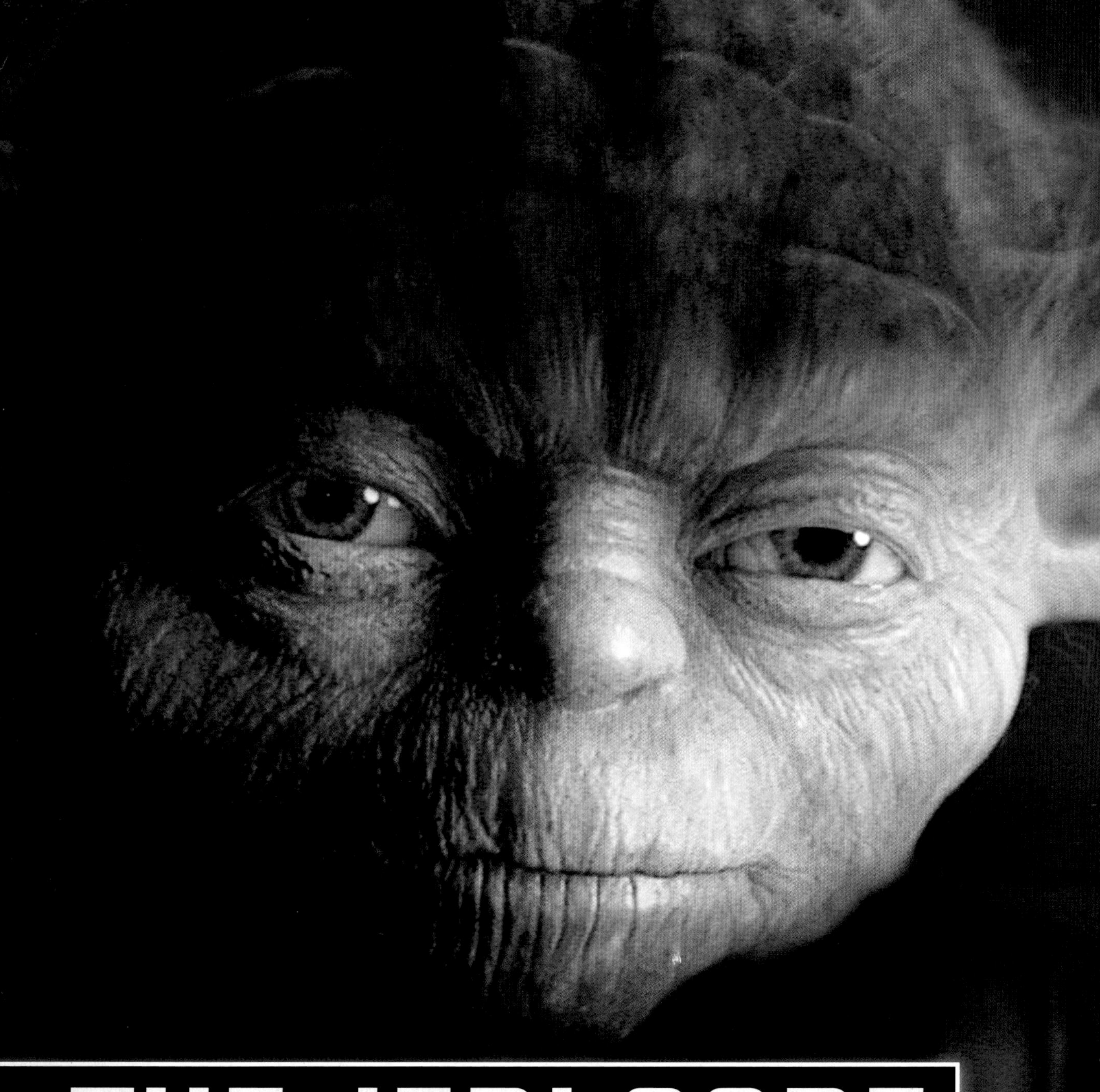

THE JEDI CODE

Welcome to the Jedi Order. As a Jedi you will learn to harness great power—but you must never use it for personal gain. To live the life of a Jedi, you will need to follow the Jedi Code. It explains the path you must take to become powerful yet remain selfless. The Jedi way of life rests on three basic principles: self-discipline, knowledge, and the Force.

SELF-DISCIPLINE

Your role as a Jedi must come before your own desires. That means having no possessions and not becoming emotionally attached: If a Jedi cares more for something or someone than he does about his mission, he might make a poor decision and jeopardize the safety of the galaxy.

THE FORCE

A Jedi must study the Force and live in tune with it. You must be able to control the Force, communicate with it, and know its will. When you interact with the Force, you will possess great power. But you must use it wisely.

KNOWLEDGE

As a Jedi, you will value knowledge and wisdom in yourself and others. You must learn how to distinguish truth from lies, and how to seek out information so you can solve problems and resolve conflict.

"THERE IS NO EMOTION, THERE IS PEACE.
THERE IS NO IGNORANCE, THERE IS KNOWLEDGE.
THERE IS NO PASSION, THERE IS SERENITY.
THERE IS NO CHAOS, THERE IS HARMONY.
THERE IS NO DEATH, THERE IS THE FORCE."

The quick-thinking Jedi blast their way out of the trap and turn the situation to their advantage. Scouting out the ship, they find a huge army and learn that Naboo is about to be invaded. They escape aboard Trade Federation transits to send warning of the attack.

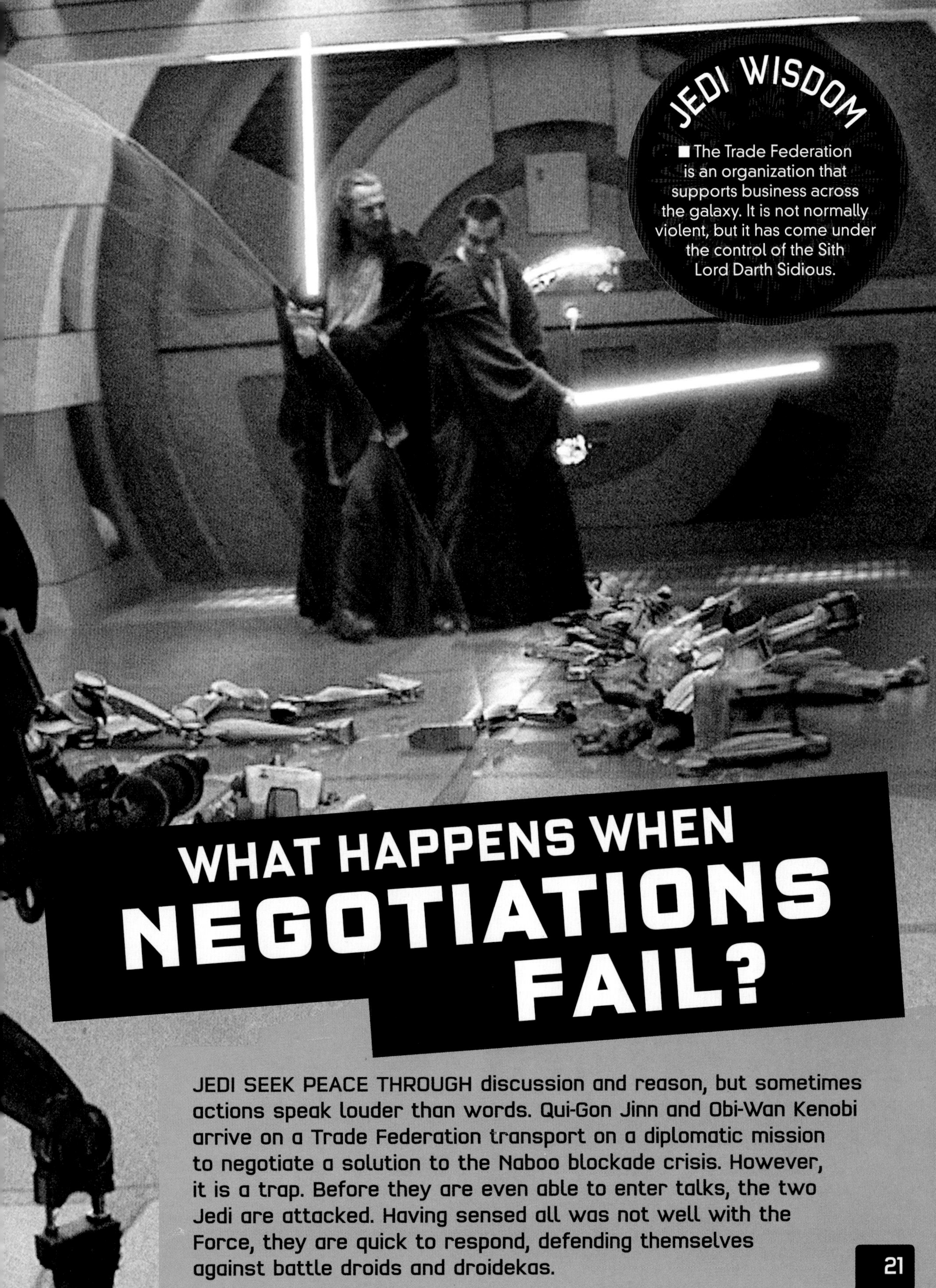

JEDI WISDOM

■ The Trade Federation is an organization that supports business across the galaxy. It is not normally violent, but it has come under the control of the Sith Lord Darth Sidious.

WHAT HAPPENS WHEN NEGOTIATIONS FAIL?

JEDI SEEK PEACE THROUGH discussion and reason, but sometimes actions speak louder than words. Qui-Gon Jinn and Obi-Wan Kenobi arrive on a Trade Federation transport on a diplomatic mission to negotiate a solution to the Naboo blockade crisis. However, it is a trap. Before they are even able to enter talks, the two Jedi are attacked. Having sensed all was not well with the Force, they are quick to respond, defending themselves against battle droids and droidekas.

HOW CAN YOU BECOME A JEDI?

Not everyone can become a Jedi: It requires dedication, hard work, and a sensitivity to the Force. It can take more than 20 years of training and there are several stages to go through. If you show promise and are selected, your Jedi career starts here. Good luck!

YOUNGLING

YOUNGLING

Great news! You have been selected to train as a Jedi. You will start as a Youngling and will live in the Jedi Temple, where you will study the basics of the Force. Most Jedi begin their training when they are babies, but some successful Jedi have started later. Get ready to work hard!

JEDI COUNCIL

The Jedi Council is made up of 12 Jedi, who are in charge of running the Jedi Order. They resolve disputes, make decisions, and uphold the Jedi Code.

GRAND MASTER YODA

GRAND MASTER

You'll have to be right at the top of your game to reach this rank. As Grand Master, Yoda is the head of not just the Jedi High Council, but the whole Order. Along with other Council members, he selects who will become Younglings.

JEDI WISDOM

■ Traditionally, those not chosen as Padawans by the age of 13 move into areas like agriculture or medicine. However, the perils of the Clone Wars force the Jedi to take on older Padawans.

PADAWAN ANAKIN SKYWALKER

JEDI TRIALS

When your Master thinks you have finished your training as a Padawan, you will sit the Jedi Trials. These grueling tasks will push you to your limits to prove you are ready for Jedi Knighthood.

PADAWAN

Well done! You have excelled as a Youngling and have been selected by a Jedi to be their Padawan. From now on, you will travel with your Master and get one-to-one training from them. Going on missions is dangerous, but it's the best way to learn.

JEDI KNIGHT AAYLA SECURA

JEDI KNIGHT

Congratulations! You must have shown great courage and strength in the Jedi Trials because you passed and are a qualified Jedi Knight. Now you can go on your own missions and even train your own Padawan.

JEDI MASTER LUMINARA UNDULI

JEDI MASTER

Once you have trained your own Padawan, you may be promoted to Jedi Master. As a Master, you will continue the duties of a Jedi and can choose another Padawan. If you show exceptional devotion and skill, you may be invited to sit on the Jedi High Council—a great honor.

WHY SHOULD A PADAWAN LISTEN TO HIS MASTER?

Anakin's impulsive attack gives Count Dooku the chance to overpower him and Obi-Wan easily. Anakin's haste also costs him his arm when Dooku's lightsaber slices it off.

Yoda arrives just in time to save Obi-Wan and Anakin, but Dooku escapes, taking with him plans for a superweapon called the Death Star. The Jedi miss the chance to learn more about their mysterious Sith enemy, to end the Clone Wars before they have really begun, and to prevent the building of the Death Star, partially because Anakin failed to heed Obi-Wan.

JEDI IN TRAINING do not study only in safe classrooms. They face real cases of life and death, with only the experience and wisdom of their Masters to guide them. When Obi-Wan and Anakin face Count Dooku, Obi-Wan knows they should fight him together. But the Padawan's anger makes him rush to attack the Sith.

WHO TAUGHT WHO?

LEARNING THE JEDI ARTS isn't easy! Every young Padawan is teamed up with a Jedi Master who shares his or her wisdom and experience with them. For centuries, skills have been passed from generation to generation as Padawans become Masters and then take on their own Padawans.

THE JEDI ▶

Ki-Adi-Mundi

Ki-Adi-Mundi began Jedi training at the age of four, which was considered late. However, thanks to his skill, dedication, and guidance from Yoda, he caught up with his peers and became a good Jedi.

YODA

Yoda has been training Jedi for centuries. This natural teacher is dedicated to helping those who want to learn, but he expects complete commitment from them in return. He is quick to point out a student's shortcomings, but also offers guidance on how to overcome them.

Count Dooku

Count Dooku often expressed controversial ideas about the Jedi Order. After his training with Master Yoda, Dooku passed on his unconventional views to his own Padawan, the young Qui-Gon Jinn.

THE SITH ▶

DARTH SIDIOUS

DARTH PLAGUEIS

Sith also follow a Master/pupil system, but the Rule of Two states that there may be only two Sith at a time. When Darth Sidious murdered his Master, the mysterious Darth Plagueis, he then searched for his own Apprentice.

Darth Maul

From a young age, Darth Maul was trained as Sidious's Apprentice in secret. He revealed his existence to the Jedi, which eventually led to his death.

Not all teachings begin with Yoda. There are many strands of Masters and Padawans. They represent ancient lines of Jedi wisdom that are still being passed on today. Here are just a few.

YADDLE

Oppo Rancisis

MACE WINDU

Depa Billaba

LUMINARA UNDULI

Barriss Offee

CLOSE BONDS

It is an honor to pass on your skills to young Jedi. However, it's not always easy. Masters don't just teach Padawans facts, they must mold their characters with Jedi values, develop their skills, and take care of them in dangerous situations. In these intense relationships, Jedi often form strong bonds that last beyond training.

Qui-Gon Jinn

Qui-Gon was rebellious and outspoken, but he was loyal to the Jedi Order—unlike his former Master, Count Dooku. Qui-Gon's Padawan, Obi-Wan Kenobi, often disagreed with Qui-Gon's opinions, but he also respected Qui-Gon's wisdom and skill.

Obi-Wan Kenobi

At first Obi-Wan struggled to find a Master due to his rash temperament. However, thanks to Qui-Gon's patience and guidance, Obi-Wan became a model Jedi. As Qui-Gon was dying, he made Obi-Wan promise to train Anakin Skywalker.

Anakin Skywalker

Anakin and Obi-Wan developed a very close bond, even though Anakin didn't always agree with his Master. Anakin was often difficult and stubborn, so when he was assigned a Padawan he was given someone equally as stubborn. Anakin learned a lot about teaching when he trained Ahsoka Tano.

Ahsoka Tano

Ahsoka was proud to be Anakin's Padawan. Although their strong personalities clashed at first, they went on to develop a great relationship.

Luke Skywalker

Under the Empire, after the Jedi Purge, the Jedi arts were at risk of being lost. Through Luke, they were preserved and went on to flourish.

Darth Tyranus

For his next Apprentice, Darth Sidious chose the Jedi Count Dooku. He tempted him over to the dark side with promises of great power. Dooku took the Sith name Darth Tyranus, but was ultimately betrayed by Sidious to make way for his next Apprentice, Darth Vader.

Darth Vader

Darth Sidious set his sights on another Jedi for his next Apprentice—Anakin Skywalker. Anakin eventually turned to the dark side and took the name Darth Vader.

MECHANICALLY MINDED
From an early age, Anakin had a knack for seeing how things work. He often tinkered with gadgets for fun. Without being taught, he built his own protocol droid, called C-3PO, from spare parts.

TALENTED

Anakin has the ability to become a great Jedi. He is brave, heroic, and dedicated, and has a strong sense of justice. Yet he struggles to control his emotions in the way a Jedi should. Sometimes he is impulsive and acts out of anger, revenge, or pride, which gets him into trouble.

JEDI STATS

SPECIES: HUMAN
HOMEWORLD: TATOOINE
BIRTHDATE: 41 BBY
HEIGHT: 1.85 M (6 FT)
RANK: JEDI KNIGHT
TRAINED BY: OBI-WAN KENOBI
WEAPON: BLUE-BLADED LIGHTSABER
PREFERRED COMBAT STYLE: FORM V (SHIEN/DJEM SO)
KNOWN FOR: HEROIC FEATS

Anakin's fighting style uses strong, powerful attacks. As a Padawan, however, he underestimates Count Dooku—which costs him his arm.

Anakin SKYWALKER

As a young boy, Anakin discovers that he is the Chosen One who will bring balance to the Force. But prophecies do not always play out as expected. Anakin has the potential to be the most skilled Jedi ever known, but only he can determine his future.

SHOW-OFF

Anakin is good at being a Jedi—and he knows it. He likes proving that he is better than his Master Obi-Wan, whether he's finding a better way to catch an assassin or flying super fast.

HOW CAN A HUMAN SURVIVE A PODRACE?

JEDI WISDOM

■ Some aliens are good Podracers because they have super-fast reflexes, but it doesn't mean they have the other skills needed to be a Jedi.

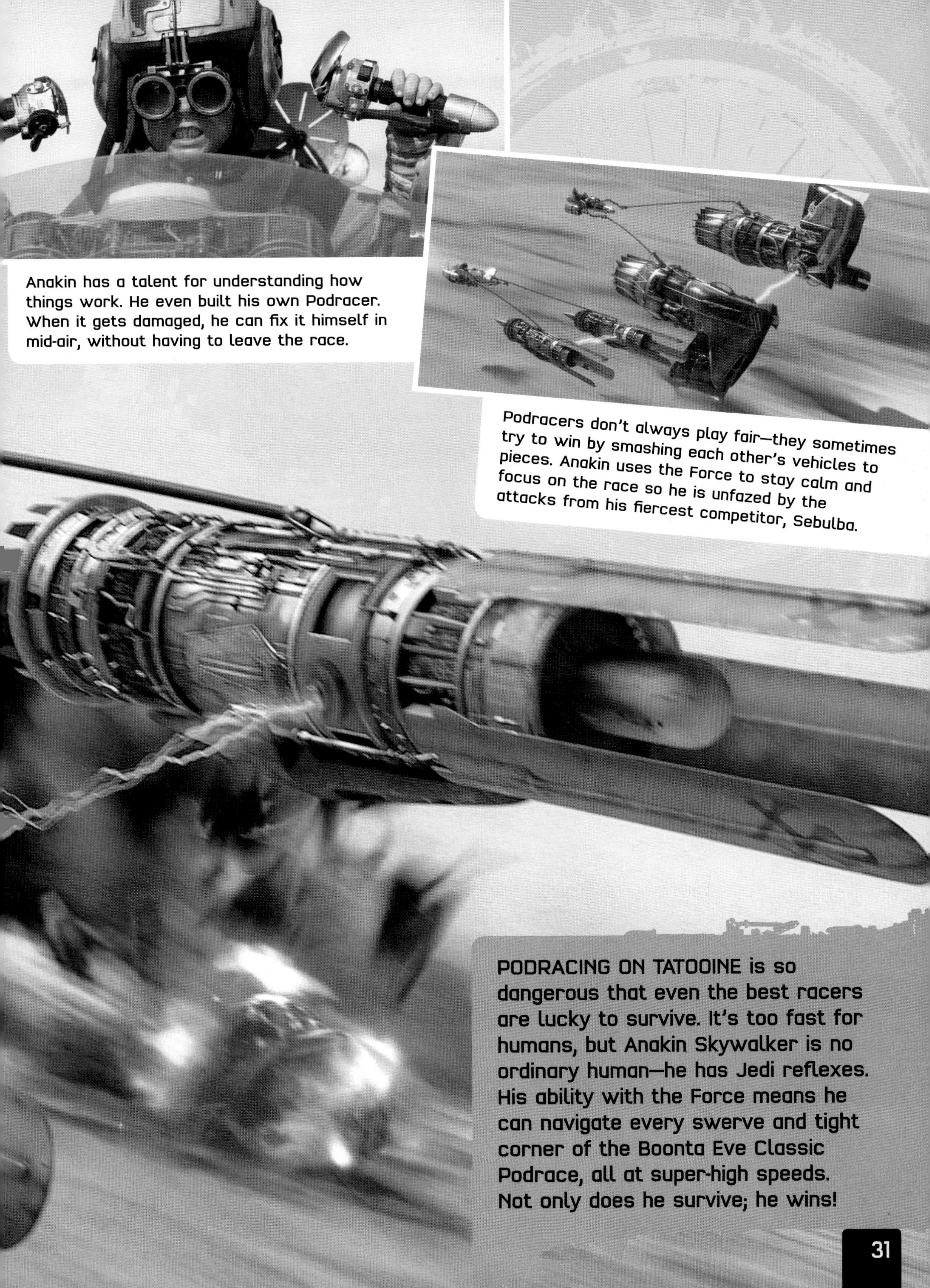

Anakin has a talent for understanding how things work. He even built his own Podracer. When it gets damaged, he can fix it himself in mid-air, without having to leave the race.

Podracers don't always play fair—they sometimes try to win by smashing each other's vehicles to pieces. Anakin uses the Force to stay calm and focus on the race so he is unfazed by the attacks from his fiercest competitor, Sebulba.

PODRACING ON TATOOINE is so dangerous that even the best racers are lucky to survive. It's too fast for humans, but Anakin Skywalker is no ordinary human—he has Jedi reflexes. His ability with the Force means he can navigate every swerve and tight corner of the Boonta Eve Classic Podrace, all at super-high speeds. Not only does he survive; he wins!

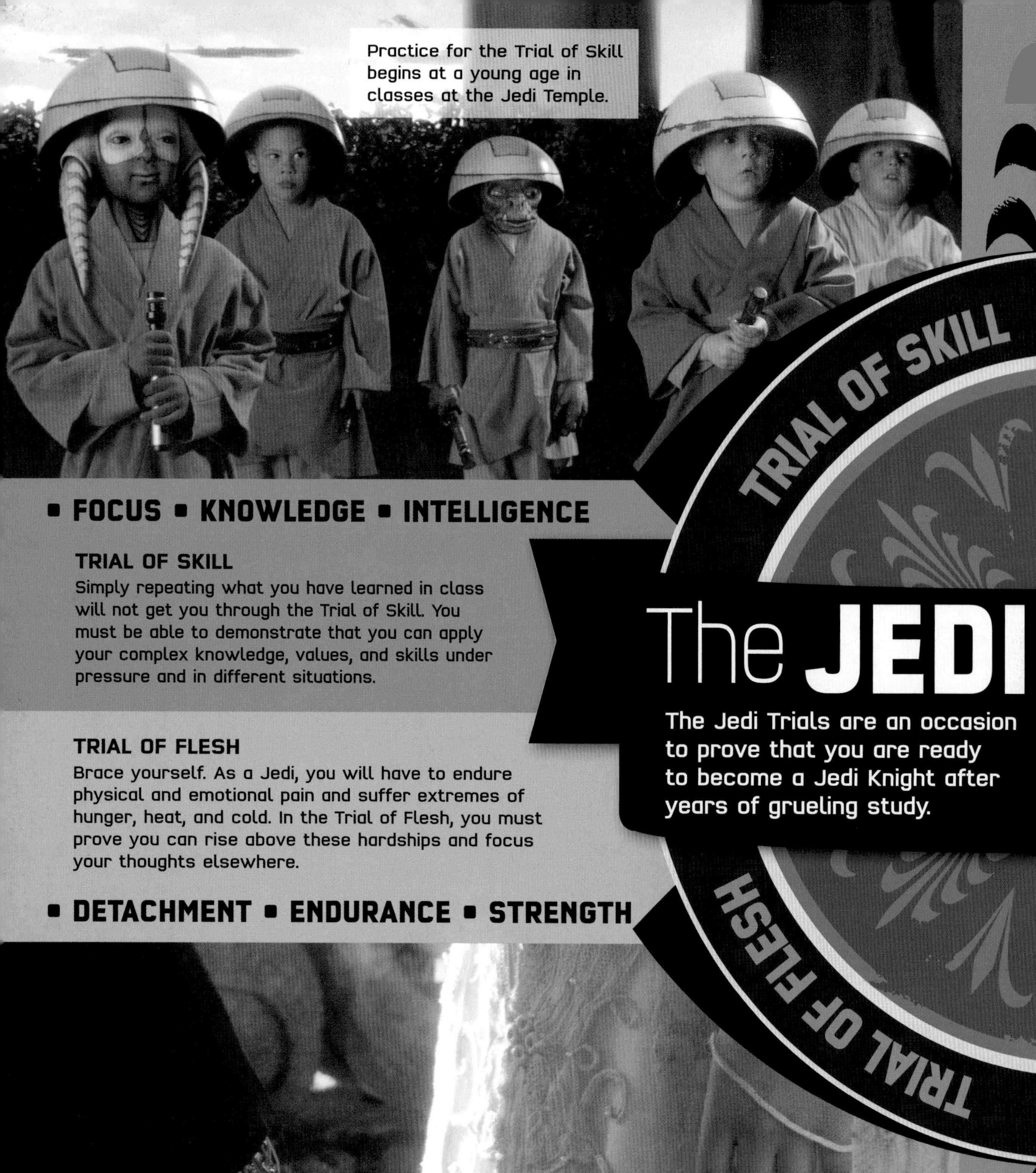

Practice for the Trial of Skill begins at a young age in classes at the Jedi Temple.

• FOCUS • KNOWLEDGE • INTELLIGENCE

TRIAL OF SKILL

Simply repeating what you have learned in class will not get you through the Trial of Skill. You must be able to demonstrate that you can apply your complex knowledge, values, and skills under pressure and in different situations.

The JEDI

The Jedi Trials are an occasion to prove that you are ready to become a Jedi Knight after years of grueling study.

TRIAL OF FLESH

Brace yourself. As a Jedi, you will have to endure physical and emotional pain and suffer extremes of hunger, heat, and cold. In the Trial of Flesh, you must prove you can rise above these hardships and focus your thoughts elsewhere.

• DETACHMENT • ENDURANCE • STRENGTH

Anakin experiences his Trial of Flesh when he loses part of his arm, including his hand, in combat with Count Dooku. From then on, he has a mechanical hand.

Obi-Wan shows bravery worthy of a Trial of Courage when he takes on Darth Maul in one-to-one combat.

TRIALS

The four trials are not easy. They are designed to push you to—and beyond—your physical, mental, and emotional limits.

• BRAVERY • COMBAT SKILLS • VALOR

TRIAL OF COURAGE

Facing death is all in a day's work for a Jedi. You must be able to control your fear and channel it into useful actions. The Trial of Courage separates those who dare from those who dare not.

TRIAL OF SPIRIT

Being a Jedi is not just a job—it's a state of mind. You must meditate on who you are and check that your motivations are pure. The Trial of Spirit forces you to look deep inside yourself and address any weaknesses or shortcomings.

• MASTERY OF EMOTIONS • LOYALTY
• MEDITATION

On Dagobah, Luke undergoes his Trial of Spirit in a vision where he battles Darth Vader. He struggles with his own dark powers, and fails. Will he turn to the dark side?

A Jedi needs to be very skilled with a lightsaber, but also lucky. Qui-Gon's luck runs out against the Sith Lord Darth Maul, but he meets his death valiantly.

MAVERICK

Qui-Gon is quick to speak his mind. He believes in the Jedi way, but his interpretation of it sometimes brings him into conflict with the Jedi Council. This rebellious streak has cost him a seat on the Council. However, Qui-Gon is not interested in politics; he prefers to be true to himself.

Qui-Gon JINN

Qui-Gon is a wise and powerful Jedi Master. He follows the values of the Jedi Code, but is not afraid to think for himself. He is very conscious of the living Force and is mindful of its will. Qui-Gon likes to live in the moment and focus on the present.

JEDI STATS

SPECIES: HUMAN
HOMEWORLD: UNKNOWN
BIRTHDATE: 92 BBY
HEIGHT: 1.93 M (6 FT 4 IN)
RANK: JEDI MASTER
TRAINED BY: COUNT DOOKU
WEAPON: GREEN-BLADED LIGHTSABER
PREFERRED COMBAT STYLE: FORM IV (ATARU)
TRADEMARK: MAVERICK

WELL-WORN JEDI ROBE
LONG HAIR IS A SIGN OF HIS REBELLIOUS NATURE

ALL HEART

Qui-Gon has a compassionate nature that often spurs him to go beyond the call of duty to help others. On Naboo, he speaks up to save Jar Jar Binks from certain death. In return, the grateful Gungan gives Qui-Gon his loyalty and service, which prove invaluable for the Jedi during the Battle of Naboo.

DETERMINED

Qui-Gon is very self-assured in his opinions. When he finds Anakin on Tatooine, he is convinced that the slave boy is the Chosen One. Qui-Gon is so sure that he risks his own ship in a bet with Anakin's greedy owner, Watto, to win the boy's freedom. He also insists that Anakin be trained as a Jedi, even though it goes against the Jedi Council.

WHAT DOES IT TAKE TO DEFEAT A SITH?

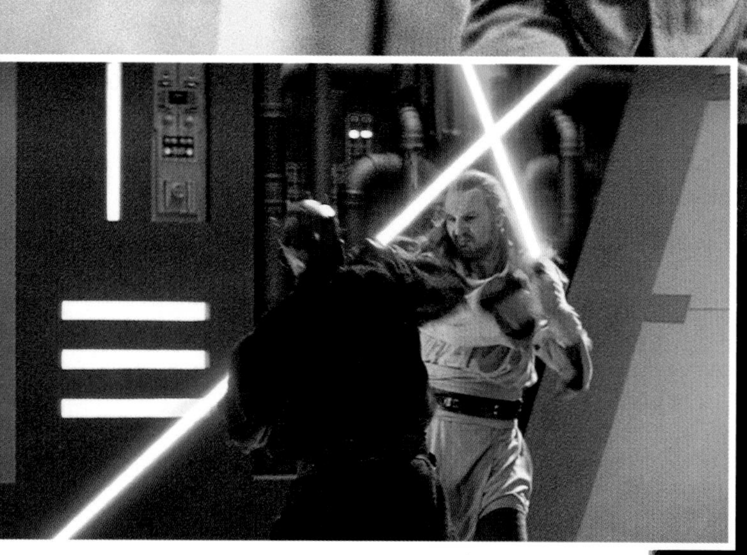

Such is Darth Maul's skill with his double-bladed lightsaber, that Qui-Gon and Obi-Wan must both dig deep to duel him. While Obi-Wan is trapped behind a laser door, Qui-Gon falters in the heat of battle and pays the ultimate price.

With his Master slain, Obi-Wan now fights Darth Maul. The Jedi appears to be at the Sith's mercy: hanging over an abyss, his weapon lost. Using his quick thinking, strength, and the element of surprise, Obi-Wan uses the Force to jump high and grab Qui-Gon's lightsaber. He defeats an unsuspecting Maul with one swift blow.

YOU CAN TELL A LOT BY A JEDI'S BODY LANGUAGE

JEDI MISSIONS ARE OFTEN highly dangerous and shrouded in secrecy. However, by paying attention to a Jedi's body language and clothing, you may pick up some clues about what they are up to.

HANDS CLASPED

Clasped hands under a cloak cannot reach easily for a weapon. Jedi stand like this on diplomatic missions as a sign of peace, service, and respect.

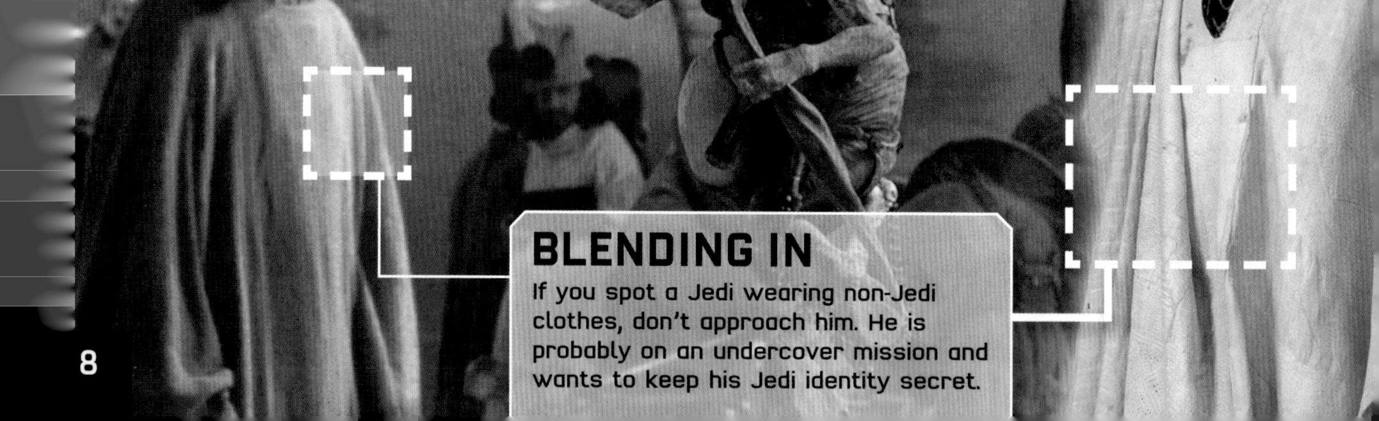

BLENDING IN

If you spot a Jedi wearing non-Jedi clothes, don't approach him. He is probably on an undercover mission and wants to keep his Jedi identity secret.

HOOD ON

If you see a Jedi with his hood on, don't disturb him—it means he's on a secret mission. A Jedi will wear his hood to help deflect attention when it's not safe for him to be out in the open.

CLOAK OFF

When you see a Jedi discard his or her cloak, get ready for action! Their long cloaks are not practical when fighting; a Jedi needs to be able to move freely.

TOUGH TASKMASTER

Luminara expects the same high standards of her Padawan and her troops as she does of herself. She is demanding and strict, but is respected so she gets the best out of people.

JEDI STATS

SPECIES: MIRIALAN

HOMEWORLD: MIRIAL

BIRTHDATE: 58 BBY

HEIGHT: 1.70 M (5 FT 7 IN)

RANK: JEDI MASTER

TRAINED BY: UNKNOWN

PREFERRED COMBAT STYLE: FORM III (SORESU)

TRADEMARK: ADHERENCE TO RULES

HUMBLE ADVISOR
Luminara is a trusted contributor to the Jedi Council, but is mindful of her position. She stands back respectfully and offers her opinion only when asked for it.

Luminara UNDULI

Jedi Master Luminara Unduli is a stickler for the rules. As far as she's concerned, there's little room in the Jedi Code for self-expression. For her, the cornerstones of the Jedi Order are discipline, discipline, discipline.

FLOWING MIRIALAN ROBES

JEDI STATS

SPECIES: MIRIALAN

HOMEWORLD: MIRIAL

BIRTHDATE: 40 BBY

HEIGHT: 1.66 M (5 FT 5 IN)

RANK: JEDI KNIGHT

TRAINED BY: LUMINARA UNDULI

PREFERRED COMBAT STYLE: FORM III (SORESU)

TRADEMARK: RESPONSIBILITY

A HEALING FORCE

Barriss has a strong connection to the Force. This helps her wield her lightsaber like a pro. But even more valuable in the middle of war, Barriss is an expert at using the Force to heal sick or injured people.

Barriss OFFEE

Barriss Offee is a model Padawan. She is loyal, obedient, and respectful to her strict Master, Luminara Unduli. After earning her knighthood during the Clone Wars, she continues to serve alongside Luminara.

MIRIALAN TATTOOS

STEPPING UP

Barriss is only a Padawan when she is flung into the Clone Wars. Her lightsaber skills and cool head help her rise to meet the challenge.

HOW TO BUILD A LIGHTSABER

THE LIGHTSABER is an ancient sword known for its elegance as well as its power in battle. It is the weapon of choice for both the Jedi and their enemies, the Sith. Lightsabers consist of a handle, or "hilt," that emits a colored blade of plasma energy. As part of their training, every Jedi learns how to build their own lightsaber. All lightsabers contain these eight basic parts, but you can vary the design to suit your own taste and needs.

JEDI WISDOM

During the Knighting Ceremony when a Padawan becomes a Knight, a lightsaber is used to cut off the Padawan's braid.

MAIN HILT

The plasma for the blade is created here in the blade energy channel from a special type of gas.

BLADE EMITTER

This is where the plasma blade beams out. The metal ring houses the base of the blade and makes sure it keeps its cylindrical shape.

FOCUSING LENS

The focusing lens channels the plasma for the blade and makes sure it has a fixed end point. Most blades are one meter (3¼ feet) long, but they can vary.

BLADE ENERGY CHANNEL

CRYSTAL

A crystal sits at the heart of every lightsaber and gives the blade its bright color. Most Jedi lightsabers glow blue or green because they use crystals mined on the planet Ilum. The Sith prefer to make their own artificial crystals so their blades glow a more fearsome red color.

The crystal also determines the length of the blade. Having more than one crystal means you can vary the length of your blade. Many Jedi believe that three is best number of crystals to have.

POWER CELL

Energy from special diatium batteries stored in the power cell heats up gas to create plasma for the blade.

POMMEL CAP

The pommel seals the end of the lightsaber. It often contains a back-up battery. If you want, you can add a ring that clips to your belt.

CONTROLS

Buttons activate the blade, but Jedi who are very skilled in the Force can control these things using the Force instead.

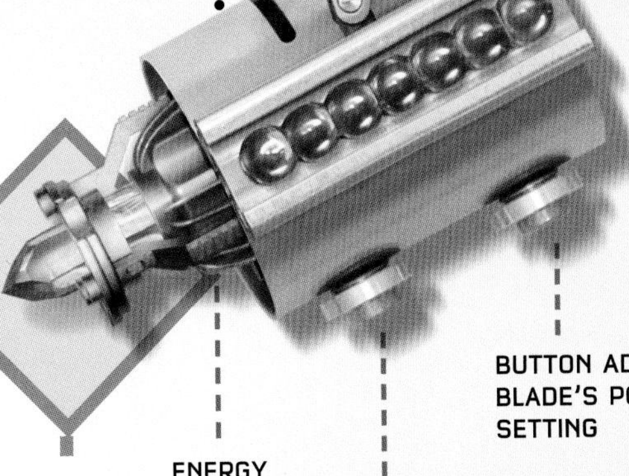

ENERGY GATE

BUTTON ADJUSTS BLADE'S LENGTH

BUTTON ADJUSTS BLADE'S POWER SETTING

HANDGRIP

This outer part of the hilt is covered in ridges so that the lightsaber doesn't fly out of your hand while you are swinging it around.

DOS AND DON'TS

- Don't plunge your blade into water—it will sizzle out unless it has been specially adapted to work underwater.
- Take care of your lightsaber —if you lose it, it can take a month to build a new one.
- Make sure your power cell is covered with an inert power insulator, otherwise you could get electrocuted!
- Keep fit: The forces acting on the weightless blade mean that a lightsaber requires strong arms to control it.
- Study the Force: Anyone can wield a lightsaber, but only those with Force powers can unlock its true potential.
- Be careful: The blade can slice through almost anything. (Any injuries you get won't bleed because the blade is so hot it seals the skin, but that doesn't mean they won't hurt!)
- Keep your lightsaber in good condition and it could last forever and never run out of power.

WHAT HAPPENS WHEN A CYBORG STUDIES JEDI SKILLS?

General Grievous is a fearsome fighter, and his lightsabers make him all the more deadly. But he doesn't understand the Force. Obi-Wan shows him that four lightsabers are no match for one lightsaber wielded by a true Jedi.

Grievous thinks he is better than the Jedi. However, no Jedi thinks himself above anyone. Grievous's arrogance is his downfall. Obi-Wan struggles in their duel, but in the end, his emotional detachment brings him victory.

COUNT DOOKU HAS trained General Grievous in the Jedi arts. These lightsaber skills have made the part-machine, part-organic warrior even more dangerous. However, just being able to wield a lightsaber doesn't make him a Jedi. Not that he wants to be a Jedi: Grievous likes nothing better than killing Jedi and adding their lightsabers to his creepy collection.

JEDI WISDOM

■ General Grievous was a reptilian Kaleesh warrior who was injured in battle. Now all that remains of his body are his brain and the organs encased in his metal chest.

HOW DO YOU FIGHT WITH A LIGHTSABER?

Wielding a lightsaber may look easy, but it is a difficult skill that requires much training. There are seven main forms of lightsaber combat. Every Jedi has a favorite, but the most skilled can switch between all the styles depending on the situation.

TRAINING HELMET

SHII-CHO BASIC STANCE

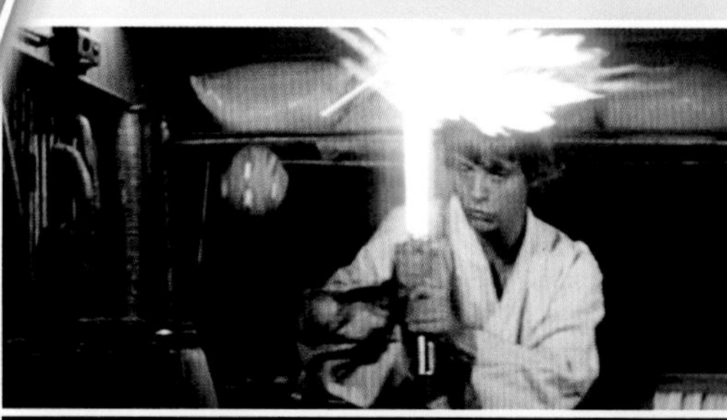

Luke begins with Shii-Cho as a way of learning to channel the Force and master his lightsaber. This exercise involves deflecting blasts from a training remote.

FORM I: SHII-CHO

When trainee Jedi get their lightsabers, the first thing they learn is Form I. It introduces them to all the basic parts of lightsaber combat: how to attack and how to defend or "parry." To master it properly, Younglings practice all the steps again and again in drills known as "velocities."

ALSO KNOWN AS: Way of the Sarlacc or Determination Form

FORM II: MAKASHI

Makashi is a development of Shii-Cho that is designed for lightsaber-to-lightsaber duels. Precision and discipline are key to Makashi, rather than strength or power. The style requires very accurate bladework and elegant, well-balanced footwork.

ALSO KNOWN AS: Way of the Ysalamir or Contention Form

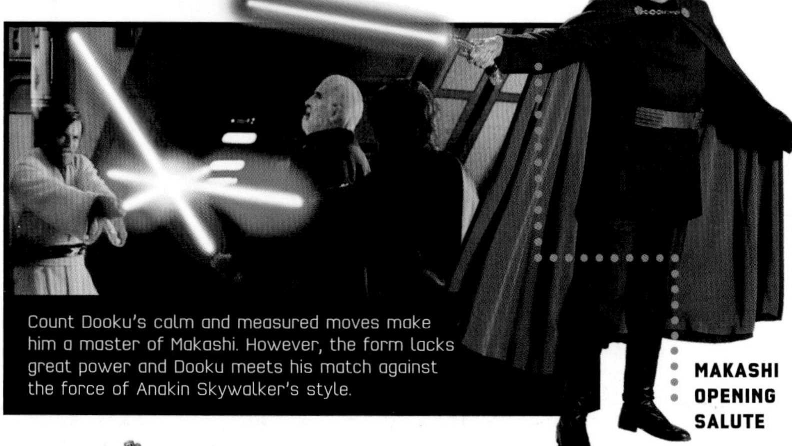

Count Dooku's calm and measured moves make him a master of Makashi. However, the form lacks great power and Dooku meets his match against the force of Anakin Skywalker's style.

MAKASHI OPENING SALUTE

BLADE PROTECTS BODY

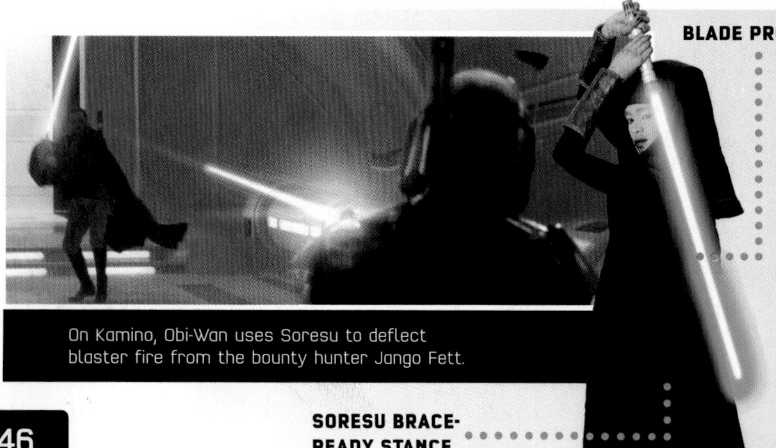

On Kamino, Obi-Wan uses Soresu to deflect blaster fire from the bounty hunter Jango Fett.

SORESU BRACE-READY STANCE

FORM III: SORESU

For Jedi who find themselves under blaster attack, then Soresu is a good choice. It is the most defensive of the seven forms. The idea is to make only small movements and keep the blade close to the body to give the best protection from blaster fire. Although Soresu is defensive, it does not have to be passive: Jedi sometimes defend themselves until their opponent tires—then they attack.

ALSO KNOWN AS: Way of the Mynock or Resilience Form

FORM IV: ATARU

For agile and athletic Jedi, Ataru is a good option. Masters of this form use acrobatic jumps, twirls, and twists to drive power into their bold attacks. It's also handy for short Jedi like Yoda who want to add height to their reach. Furthermore, it's useful for confusing and distracting your opponent.

ALSO KNOWN AS: Way of the Hawk-Bat or Aggression Form

Obi-Wan uses his mastery of Ataru along with the Force to add great power to his lightsaber moves.

ATARU PRE-JUMP STANCE

Anakin is very strong and he uses this power to drive aggression into his Djem So attacks.

DJEM SO OPENING STANCE

FORM V: SHIEN/DJEM SO

The two versions of Form V developed out of Form III to combine aggression with the defensive style. Shien is used for redirecting blaster bolts back at the person who fired them. Djem-So is used to push back another lightsaber during a duel. Whichever a Jedi chooses, they must be strong and fit so their deflective moves really pack a punch.

ALSO KNOWN AS: Way of the Krayt Dragon or Perseverance Form

FORM VI: NIMAN

Niman is about balance and harmony rather than aggressive power. It is a good choice for Jedi who are less experienced in battle because it is less demanding than the other forms. It covers the basic moves, but is too general for some situations so is often used with other Force powers like telekinesis.

ALSO KNOWN AS: Way of the Rancor or Moderation Form

Niman is very popular during the Battle of Geonosis among Jedi like Joclad Danva.

NIMAN OPENING STANCE

VAAPAD OPENING STANCE

Mace is one of the few Jedi strong enough to use dark feelings without falling to the dark side.

FORM VII: JUYO/VAAPAD

If a Jedi is super-energetic, then the big, direct moves of Form VII could be their best option. But this style comes with a warning: Form VII can be dangerous because it taps into powerful emotions that can open a Jedi up to the dark side. Juyo is the original version. Vaapad is a variant developed by the Jedi Master Mace Windu that particularly focuses on a Jedi's state of mind.

ALSO KNOWN AS: Way of Vornskr or Ferocity Form

Anakin Skywalker's Lightsaber

This lightsaber is passed from Anakin to Luke. It is lost when Luke fights Darth Vader on Cloud City.

Mace Windu's Lightsaber

Mace's hilt is plated with golden electrum metal—a decoration reserved for senior Jedi.

Mace chooses a rare crystal that emits a violet glow.

Luke Skywalker's Lightsaber

After Luke loses his first lightsaber fighting Darth Vader, he builds a new one using notes left by Obi-Wan.

Youngling Lightsaber

Younglings practice with safety blades. The power setting is very low to avoid injuries.

"Your lightsaber is ...YOUR LIFE!"

OBI-WAN TO ANAKIN

Darth Maul's Lightsaber

The Sith Darth Maul chooses a saberstaff, which is double-bladed. These are harder to use, but some Sith favor them because they look more menacing and allow a more aggressive style of combat.

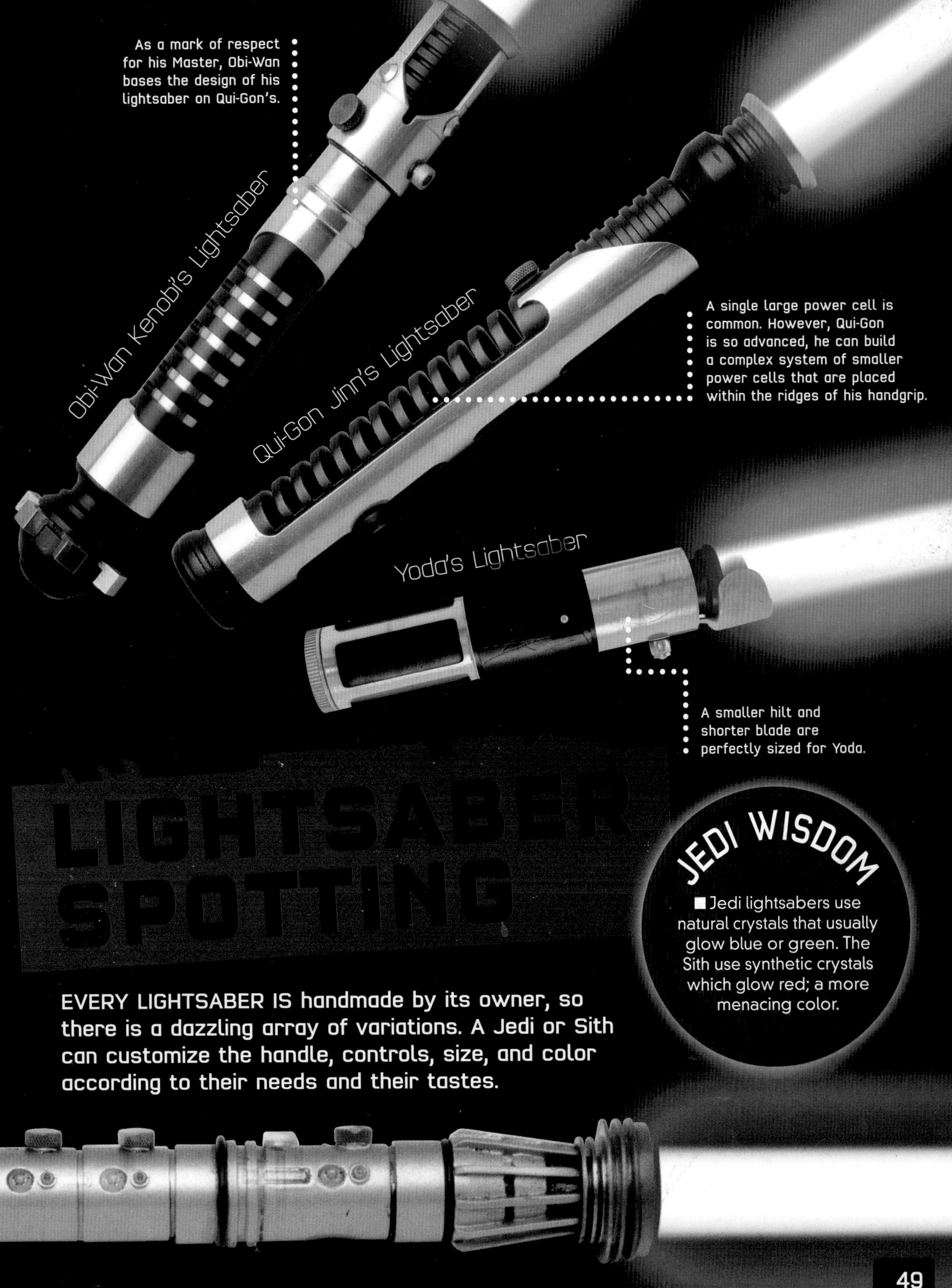
As a mark of respect for his Master, Obi-Wan bases the design of his lightsaber on Qui-Gon's.
Obi-Wan Kenobi's Lightsaber
Qui-Gon Jinn's Lightsaber
A single large power cell is common. However, Qui-Gon is so advanced, he can build a complex system of smaller power cells that are placed within the ridges of his handgrip.
Yoda's Lightsaber
A smaller hilt and shorter blade are perfectly sized for Yoda.

LIGHTSABER SPOTTING

JEDI WISDOM

■ Jedi lightsabers use natural crystals that usually glow blue or green. The Sith use synthetic crystals which glow red; a more menacing color.

EVERY LIGHTSABER IS handmade by its owner, so there is a dazzling array of variations. A Jedi or Sith can customize the handle, controls, size, and color according to their needs and their tastes.

Aayla SECURA

JEDI STATS

SPECIES: TWI'LEK
HOMEWORLD: RYLOTH
BIRTHDATE: UNKNOWN
HEIGHT: 1.78 M (5 FT 10 IN)
RANK: JEDI MASTER
TRAINED BY: QUINLAN VOS & THOLME
PREFERRED COMBAT STYLE: FORM IV (ATARU) & FORM V (SHIEN/DJEM SO)
TRADEMARK: EMPATHY

RUTIAN SKIN COLOR

BRUSH WITH EVIL

Aayla knows first hand what the temptations of the dark side can be. In her youth, she struggled with dark powers, but this has made her stronger. She is a more determined Jedi as a result.

LEKKU (HEAD TAILS) CAN EXPRESS EMOTIONS

RESPECTED

Aayla's skill and easy-going nature make her a popular General during the Clone Wars. She soon rises to the rank of Master. However, her career is brought to a swift end when she is killed in the Jedi Purge.

Aayla Secura is a talented Twi'lek Jedi with distinctive blue skin. Her quick thinking has saved many lives. She brings a light-hearted and mischievous approach to the serious business of being a Jedi.

KI-ADI-MUNDI

As a Cerean, Ki-Adi-Mundi believes in a simple way of life, and this simplicity serves him well as a Jedi. His large Cerean brain gives him extra thinking power and earns him a well-deserved seat on the Jedi High Council.

LARGE BINARY BRAIN

BODY HAS TWO HEARTS TO SUPPORT LARGE BRAIN

BRAINY GENERAL
The outbreak of the Clone Wars sees Ki-Adi-Mundi's insightful and logical mind put to work on the battlefield. He leads his troops with honor and survives the conflict, only to die in the Jedi Purge.

JEDI STATS

SPECIES: CEREAN

HOMEWORLD: CEREA

BIRTHDATE: 92 BBY

HEIGHT: 1.98 M (6 FT 6 IN)

RANK: JEDI MASTER

TRAINED BY: YODA

PREFERRED COMBAT STYLE: FORM III (SORESU)

TRADEMARK: INTELLIGENCE

FAMILY MAN

Although Jedi are not allowed to marry or have children, a special exception is made for Ki-Adi-Mundi because the Cereans have a very low birthrate. Nevertheless, he always puts his duties as a Jedi ahead of his feelings, even when his family is killed in the Clone Wars.

THE JEDI TEMPLE TOUR

The Jedi Temple stands out on Coruscant thanks to its unique appearance. One of the oldest and largest buildings on the planet, the 4,000-year-old Temple has a huge, pyramid-like base and five colossal spires. It is the headquarters of the Jedi Order. Come, take the Jedi Temple Tour.

COUNCIL OF FIRST KNOWLEDGE TOWER

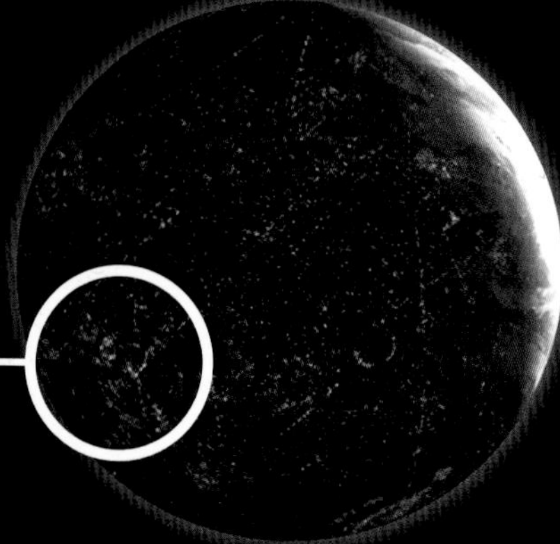

THE PLANET

Welcome to Coruscant—a planet entirely covered by a single city. You are visiting the place that is the most important political hub in the galaxy, thanks to its central location. Coruscant was the capital city of the Republic, home to the Galactic Senate, the office of the Chancellor, and, of course, the Jedi Temple. During the Emperor's reign, the planet was also home to the Imperial Palace. Enjoy your stay!

SURFACE LIFE

This planet is a bustling metropolis, full of bright lights and congested skylanes. It is home to over 1 trillion residents, made up of a multitude of races and species. Many areas are built up with beautiful, modern architecture—but be warned! A dangerous underworld lurks in the shadows. Watch out for prowling gangs who make some areas unsafe.

THE SPIRE

Look up! At the peak of the Temple's southwestern spire you can see the meeting chamber of the Jedi High Council. This airy room has 12 chairs arranged in a circle, allowing the Council members to see each other, and symbolizing that each person's opinion is equally important.

JEDI WISDOM

■ The five spires of the Jedi Temple are topped with powerful antennas that enable communication with Jedi on distant planets throughout the galaxy.

THE TEMPLE

Next stop: the Jedi Temple, home to the Jedi Order. Within these gleaming walls are training rooms, the Jedi Archives, offices, meditation chambers, bedrooms, and the Jedi Council Meeting Chamber. Only a few areas of the Jedi Temple are open to the public.

COUNCIL MEMBERS IN 32 BBY

YADDLE
Yaddle contributes wisdom, compassion, and patience to the Council.

SAESEE TIIN
Saesee is particularly valued on the Council for his skill of foresight.

KI-ADI-MUNDI
Ki-Adi-Mundi, Mace, and Yoda are the three most senior Council members.

THE JEDI HIGH COUNCIL

EVEN PIELL
Even's seriousness makes him well-suited to important Council business.

OPPO RANCISIS
Oppo believes the Council should focus on traditional ideas, not modern ones.

ADI GALLIA
Adi's intuition and network of informants strengthen the Council.

LATER COUNCIL MEMBERS

ANAKIN SKYWALKER
Chancellor Palpatine chooses Anakin to serve as his personal representative on the Council. Palpatine and the Council each want Anakin to spy on the other.

SHAAK TI
The Sith spare Shaak's life so she can report Palpatine's kidnap to the Council.

OBI-WAN KENOBI
Obi-Wan proves himself worthy of a place on the Council during the challenging Clone Wars.

COLEMAN KCAJ
Coleman follows in the footsteps of many Ongree Jedi who have sat on the Council.

YODA

Yoda is the most respected Jedi and leads the High Council.

MACE WINDU

Mace's wisdom meant he joined the Council at the very young age of only 28.

PLO KOON

Plo thinks his friend Qui-Gon Jinn deserves a seat on the Council, but the others find Qui-Gon too unpredictable.

IF YOU PROVE YOURSELF to be among the most skilled and wise Jedi, then you may be given the highest honor—a seat on the Jedi High Council. As a Council member, you will have a role in organizing the Jedi Order. There are always 12 seats and if a member dies or steps down, a new member is selected by the Council to replace them.

DEPA BILLABA

Experiencing the horrors of the Clone Wars causes Depa to turn to the dark side.

YARAEL POOF

Yarael has two brains with which to ponder Council debates.

EETH KOTH

Eeth's intelligence and insight bring clarity to Council discussions.

STASS ALLIE

Before she joined the Council, Stass had a role as an advisor to senior officials in the Republic.

COLEMAN TREBOR

Coleman is media savvy and becomes the spokesperson for the Council.

KIT FISTO

Kit's achievements in the Clone Wars earn him a seat on the Council.

AGEN KOLAR

Agen is very loyal to the Council and, like most Jedi, does not question its decisions.

JEDI WISDOM

■ There are three types of Council membership. Life members commit for life. Long-term members can step down. Limited-term members serve for a fixed period.

JEDI WISDOM

For Jedi, wisdom and knowledge are the keys to success. A mission's outcome can hinge on having the most accurate data available. Gathering information is a never-ending task. Like Obi-Wan, you must ensure your facts are reliable and up-to-date. Here are some tips to guide you on your search.

1. USE THE JEDI ARCHIVES

With its ancient collection of Holocrons and millions of holobooks, the Jedi Archives are the perfect place to start your search for knowledge. Every time a piece of information is learned by the Jedi Order, it is filed and stored in the Archives for future use.

2. DIG DEEP

Always question and analyze your data—don't take anything at face value. Once, Obi-Wan couldn't find the planet Kamino in the Archives' records. Jedi Librarian Jocasta Nu told him that meant Kamino didn't exist. Obi-Wan was not so sure—someone may have tampered with the Archives.

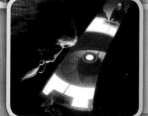

3. GO UNDERCOVER

On the trail of a tricky villain, you might have to improvise. If you can't learn the truth through simple methods, you may have to resort to spying. Obi-Wan tracked Count Dooku to Geonosis where he overheard him discussing his plans for a Death Star.

4. MAKE CONTACTS

Sometimes it's not what you know but who. Some people are happy to talk, but others may want money. You never know who might be useful. When Obi-Wan seeks information about underworld weapons, he goes to his old friend Dexter Jettster.

5. GO THE EXTRA MILE

Sometimes, all the research in the galaxy is not enough. If nobody is willing to talk, you might just have to put in lots of extra effort to get the facts. When Obi-Wan was chasing Zam Wesell for information, he risked his life by speeding through Coruscant's skylanes hanging on to an assassin droid!

Holocrons are mysterious databanks that store the deepest secrets of the Jedi. Unlike simple data files and holobooks, these ancient artifacts can be accessed only by using the Force.

Informatic stations are situated throughout the Jedi Archives. Insert a holobook into the station and it will link up with new data being accessed from all over the galaxy.

Obi-Wan Kenobi is a model Jedi. He is humble, calm, and steadfast, but can be combative when the need arises. Tutored by Qui-Gon, he passes his knowledge on to Anakin Skywalker and, later, to Anakin's son, Luke.

Obi-Wan KENOBI

JEDI STATS

SPECIES: HUMAN

HOMEWORLD: STEWJON

BIRTHDATE: 57 BBY

HEIGHT: 1.79 M (5 FT 11 IN)

RANK: JEDI MASTER

TRAINED BY: QUI-GON JINN

WEAPON: BLUE-BLADED LIGHTSABER

PREFERRED COMBAT STYLE: FORM IV (ATARU); LATER FORM III (SORESU)

TRADEMARK: NEGOTIATION

Obi-Wan is an ace with a lightsaber. When he was only a Padawan, he took on Darth Maul and his double-bladed lightsaber—and won.

HIGH HOPES

Obi-Wan sees a little of his former self in his Padawan's arrogance and impatience. This makes him believe that he can influence Anakin to be a better Jedi, as his Master, Qui-Gon, did for him.

THE NEGOTIATOR

Obi-Wan is known for his ability to resolve disputes with words and reason. People listen to him because of his charm and skills as a negotiator, but also thanks to his reputation with a lightsaber. These qualities make him a respected General in the Clone Wars.

STANDING FIRM

Obi-Wan is fiercely loyal to the Jedi Order, democracy, and justice. Even when held prisoner by Count Dooku, he refuses to join him. Nothing would make Obi-Wan turn his back on what he believes in.

Amid the chaos of the hurtling rock, clever Obi-Wan fools Jango into thinking that an exploding asteroid is his ship. Believing that he has seen Obi-Wan go up in flames, Jango zooms off, not expecting to see Obi-Wan again.

HOW DO YOU OUTWIT A BOUNTY HUNTER?

JEDI WISDOM

■ Bounty hunters do not fight for an army, but are paid on a job-by-job basis to do tasks like capturing people wanted by the Republic or the Empire.

WHEN A BOUNTY HUNTER is fighting you, he or she will not stop until the job is done and you are captured—or worse. Obi-Wan hates flying at the best of times, but now ruthless Jango Fett is gunning for him. Being a good pilot, and even steering his Delta-7 starfighter into an asteroid belt, is not enough to throw Jango. It requires something much more cunning to outwit him.

DARK SUSPICIONS
Mace has never hit it off with Anakin. Mace's deep connection with the Force means that he can sense Anakin's strong emotional attachments and so he fears for his future. Mace tries to keep Anakin in check, but the more he does this, the more he pushes Anakin away.

Mace never ignores a Jedi in trouble so he is quick to volunteer for the dangerous mission to Geonosis. The daring rescue quickly escalates into full-scale battle, but Mace's skill helps him and his troops to victory.

Mace WINDU

Across the galaxy, Mace Windu is respected for his wisdom and nobility. As a senior member of the Jedi Council, he has heavy burdens to bear. Mace has a deep knowledge of Jedi history and philosophy. When he talks, people listen.

JEDI STATS

SPECIES: HUMAN

HOMEWORLD: HARUUN KAL

BIRTHDATE: 72 BBY

HEIGHT: 1.88 M (6 FT 2 IN)

RANK: JEDI MASTER

TRAINED BY: UNKNOWN

WEAPON: VIOLET-BLADED LIGHTSABER

PREFERRED COMBAT STYLE: FORM VII (JUYO/VAAPAD)

TRADEMARK: STRENGTH

NO PUSHOVER

For Mace, the Jedi are peacekeepers, not soldiers. He likes to spend his time meditating in the Jedi Temple, but that doesn't mean he's a coward. When events force the Jedi into war, Mace is ready to stand up and fight for the things he believes in—the Republic and the Jedi Order.

BETRAYED

As a guardian of the Republic, Mace steps up to arrest Chancellor Palpatine when he learns that he is a Sith Lord. The powerful Jedi is capable of defeating Palpatine. However, Mace's misgivings about Anakin return to haunt him. Anakin steps in and Mace dies.

Jedi STARFLEET

Keeping peace across the galaxy requires wings, so piloting is a basic Jedi skill. Jedi use different types of ship depending on the needs of the mission, and some have Force-activated controls.

PRESSURIZED COCKPIT

DELTA-7 STARFIGHTER

- MAIN USE: SCOUT AND PURSUIT

This small, wedge-shaped ship is sleek and fast—ideal for keeping a low profile during enemy pursuit. Obi-Wan pilots one of these streamlined ships on his scout mission to Kamino, making use of its excellent maneuverability when pursuing the bounty hunter Jango Fett.

ANCIENT JEDI SYMBOL

LENGTH: 8 m (26 ft)
HYPERDRIVE RATING: Class 1.0
CAPACITY: 1 person

LENGTH: 5.47 m (18 ft)
HYPERDRIVE RATING: Class 1.0
CAPACITY: 1 person

ETA-2 INTERCEPTOR

- MAIN USE: COMBAT

This compact model is the Jedi ship of choice in the last years of the Republic. Adapted so Jedi pilots could use the Force instead of traditional controls, this lightweight vehicle is fast and agile. It does not have its own internal hyperdrive, so it uses an external booster ring to reach hyperspace.

SECONDARY ION CANNON

WINGS OPEN DURING INTENSE FIGHTING

LONG-BARRELED LASER CANNON

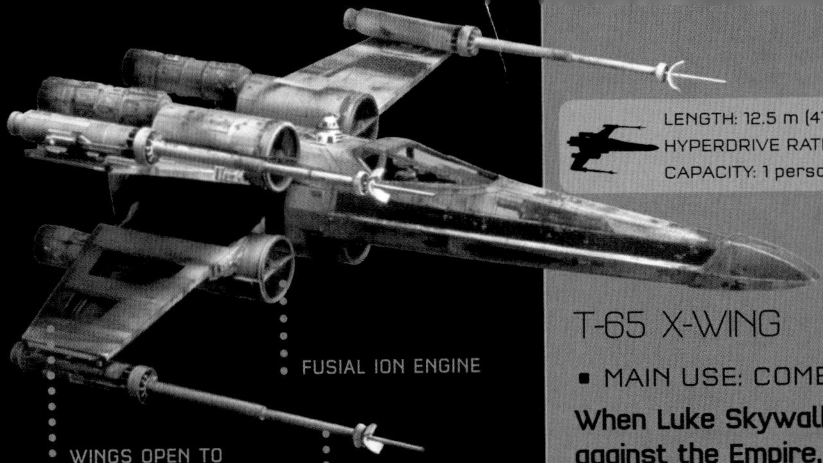

ASTROMECH DROID

FUSIAL ION ENGINE

WINGS OPEN TO MAKE "X" SHAPE

LONG-RANGE LASER CANNON

STREAMLINED HULL

LENGTH: 12.5 m (41 ft)
HYPERDRIVE RATING: Class 1.0
CAPACITY: 1 person

T-65 X-WING

- MAIN USE: COMBAT

When Luke Skywalker fights against the Empire, he flies an X-wing. This long, narrow starship boasts excellent power, balance, and stability.

Proton torpedoes and four laser cannons provide impressive firepower for a ship of this size.

BORROWED SPEED

Jedi missions are unpredictable and you can't always expect the perfect vehicle to be ready and waiting. Sometimes you have to improvise with what's available.

HOTH SNOWSPEEDER

On the icy planet of Hoth, Luke flies a T-47 snowspeeder. These agile two-seaters are civilian craft that have been adapted for battle with dual forward-facing cannons and a rear harpoon gun.

TATOOINE SWOOP BIKE

Anakin borrows Owen Lars's swoop bike for his search for his mother. This utilitarian, repulsorlift bike is perfect for the sand dunes of Tatooine.

CORUSCANT AIRSPEEDER

Anakin's choice for a high-speed chase was a good one. This open-cockpit, twin turbojet-engine luxury speeder zips through the busy traffic over Coruscant.

Anakin refuses to abandon his Master. He shunts his ship into Obi-Wan's in the hope of knocking the buzz droids off. They are all dislodged apart from one—which crawls onto Anakin's ship!

WHAT DO YOU DO WHEN BUZZ DROIDS ATTACK?

BUZZ DROIDS ARE BAD NEWS for a pilot. These small, scuttling robots cling to a ship and dismantle it from the outside in. Above Coruscant, Obi-Wan's ETA-2 Interceptor is attacked by buzz droids, which start shutting down its systems. Firing at them is no good, because it risks destroying the ship! The only way to defeat them is teamwork.

Astromech droids are perfectly positioned on the outside of ships to target buzz droids. However, Obi-Wan's astromech droid, R4-P17, is no match for them and he is pulled apart in seconds. Anakin's droid, R2-D2, is made of sterner stuff. He zaps the buzz droid right in its center eye.

Kit FISTO

SENSORY TENTA

Kit Fisto is a popular Jedi Master, respected as much for his fighting skill as for his ready smile. An easygoing Jedi, Kit values friendship as highly as he values the Jedi Code.

SENSITIVE

Kit is able to breathe in both air and water. He also has tentacles sprouting from his head, which he uses to sense the feelings of those around him. Being able to detect changing emotions enhances Kit's people skills, and gives him an edge on the battlefield.

UNBLINKING, BIG EYES GIVE EXCELLENT NIGHT VISION

LIGHTSABER ADAPTED TO BE WATERPROOF

BRAVE TO THE END

Kit Fisto is not one to stand still when villains are nearby. He joins Mace Windu on his mission to arrest Chancellor Palpatine, but is killed when Palpatine draws his lightsaber and attacks.

JEDI STATS

SPECIES: NAUTOLAN

HOMEWORLD: GLEE ANSELM

BIRTHDATE: UNKNOWN

HEIGHT: 1.96 M (6 FT 5 IN)

RANK: JEDI MASTER

TRAINED BY: UNKNOWN

PREFERRED COMBAT STYLE: FORM I (SHII-CHO)

TRADEMARK: FRIENDLINESS

JEDI STATS

SPECIES: KEL DOR

HOMEWORLD: DORIN

BIRTHDATE: UNKNOWN

HEIGHT: 1.88 M (6 FT 2 IN)

RANK: JEDI MASTER

TRAINED BY: UNKNOWN

PREFERRED COMBAT STYLE: FORM V (DJEM SO/SHIEN)

TRADEMARK: DECISIVENESS

Plo **KOON**

Plo Koon is a senior member of the Jedi Council. This stern Jedi Master is known for making fast decisions. Plo's ability to act quickly makes him both a fierce warrior and a fearsome starship pilot.

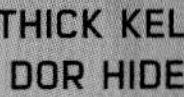

GAS MASK FOR OXYGEN-RICH ATMOSPHERES

STARFIGHTER HERO

As a Jedi General, Plo was one of the best pilots in the Republic Fleet. The mere sight of his blade-shaped starfighter terrified his enemies. But when his own troops opened fire on his ship during Order 66, Plo could do nothing to save himself.

MAN OF CONVICTION

Plo is motivated by a strict sense of right and wrong. Although he is always focused on hunting down the bad guys, he displays such concern for his troops that he has been known to risk his own life to save theirs.

THE JEDI TEMPLE is full of useful gadgets. Whether you are training a new Padawan, searching for an underwater city, taking on an AT-AT walker, or traveling to the Outer Rim, make sure you take along the right tools. You never know when they'll come in handy.

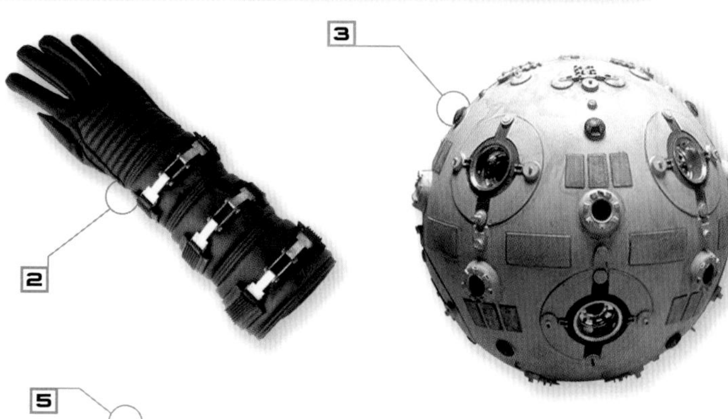

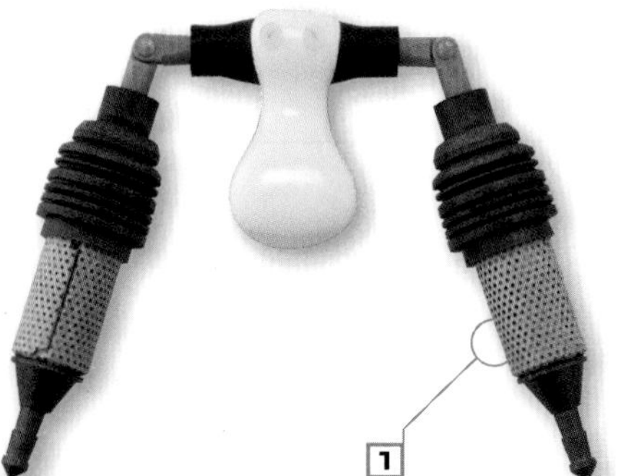

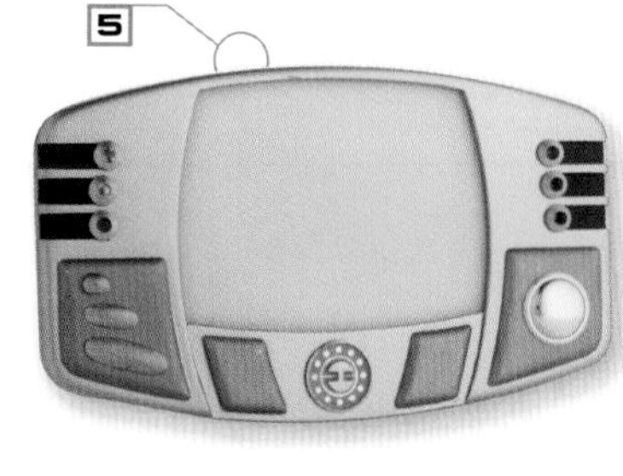

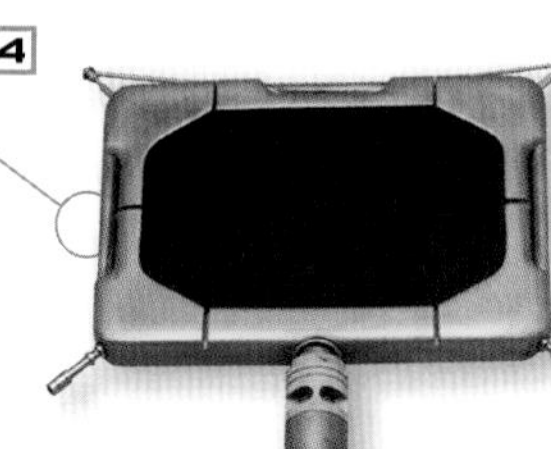

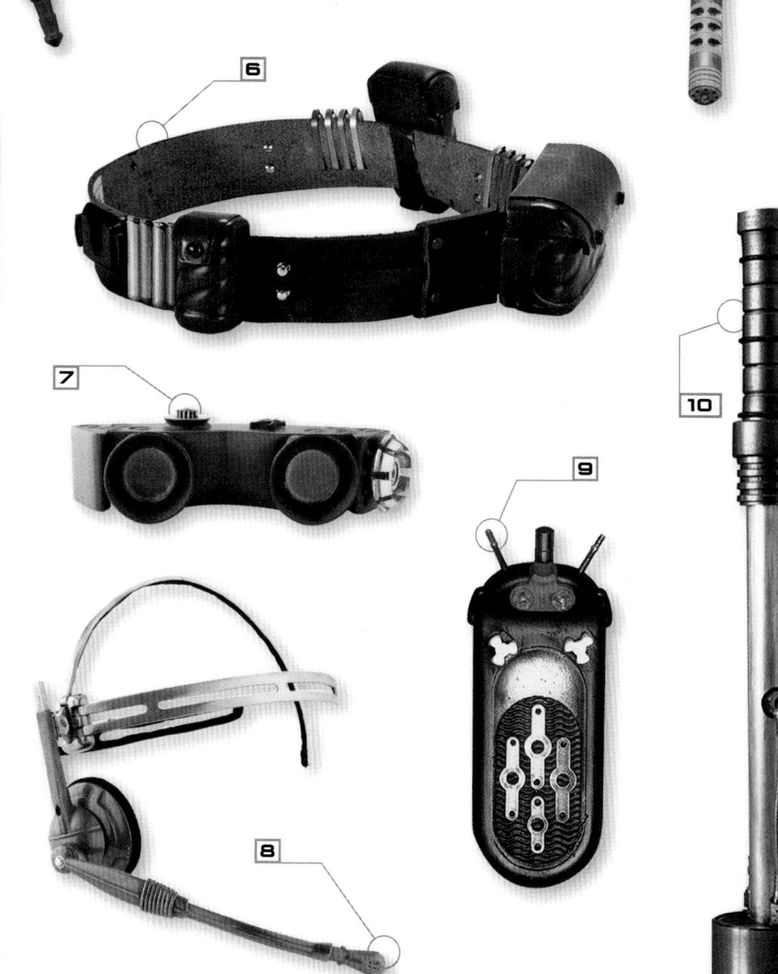

KEY

1. A99 AQUATA BREATHER to enable breathing underwater, in outer space, or in a poisonous environment.

2. Auto-seal, close fitting GLOVE to cover and protect artificial limbs.

3. TRAINING REMOTE to fire harmless beams at Padawans during lightsaber training.

4. Force-operated TESTING SCREEN to constantly challenge Padawans.

5. VIEWSCREEN to view incoming communications.

6. UTILITY BELT with storage pouches and food capsules.

7. MACROBINOCULARS for extreme long distance and outer space viewing.

8. HEADSET COMLINK to enable communication when in flight.

9. Security-enhanced COMLINK to send and receive audio messages.

10. CABLE RETRIEVER to retrieve grappling hook line.

11. TRACER BEACON to track a moving target.

12. SCANNER MONITOR to detect nearby movement, life-forms, metal, or communication signals.

13. BINOCULARS to observe long distances.

14. IMAGE ENHANCER for when transmissions are coming from exceptionally long distances.

15. HOVER CHAIR to enable easier transport within Jedi Temple.

16. TRAINING LIGHTSABER for Younglings with reduced-size hilt and low-energy blade.

17. LIGHTSABER for use during battles and duels.

18. HOLOPROJECTOR to send and receive secure, encrypted holotransmissions.

19. GRAPPLING HOOK for leaping extremely high or crossing large chasms.

20. Sturdy UTILITY POUCH with built-in grappling hook and line.

HOW CAN YOU DESTROY A DEATH STAR?

All the brave Y-wing pilots of Gold Squadron, except one, are destroyed by Imperial fire. Next, Red Squadron gets to work in their X-wings, but the mission is just too hard. Pilot after pilot is defeated, until only one remains.

The last hope lies with Luke Skywalker. But he is no ordinary pilot: The Force is strong with him. To the horror of the other Rebels, Luke switches off his tracking computer. He hears Obi-Wan telling him that if he trusts in the Force and listens to his feelings, then the Force will guide him.

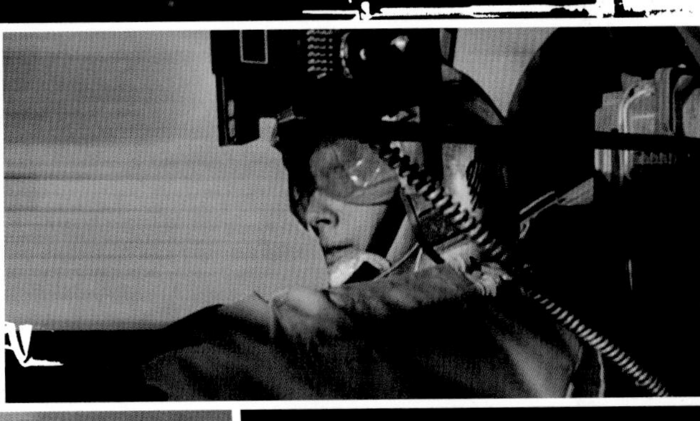

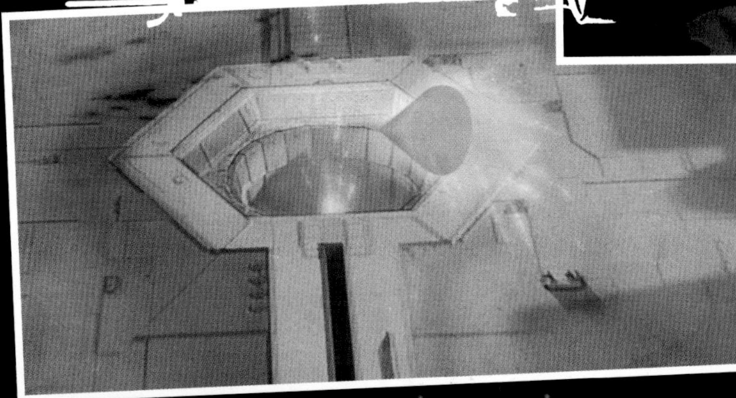

Bullseye! Luke launches the proton torpedo right on target. It begins a chain reaction that causes the whole station to explode. There's just enough time for Luke to get out of there before he is engulfed in flames.

THE GIANT ARMORED station called the Death Star is like the Empire that created it—huge, powerful, and dangerous. It seems impossible to defeat, but the resourceful Rebel Alliance has found its weakness: One direct hit on a small exhaust port opening will reduce the monster to rubble. Getting close to it, however, is no easy task.

JEDI COMRADES

The Jedi Order is made up of beings from every corner of the galaxy. Species, age, height, or gender are not important; it matters only that you are attuned to the Force and committed to the Jedi way. Every Jedi has something unique to offer the Order.

STRONG WILLED

SPECIES: THOLOTHIAN
HOMEWORLD: THOLOTH

STASS ALLIE seeks peace, but she believes that sometimes you have to fight in order to achieve it.

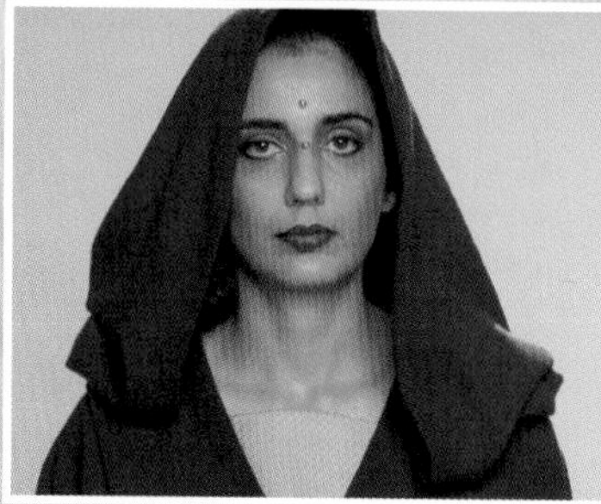

FALLEN JEDI

SPECIES: CHALACTAN
HOMEWORLD: CORUSCANT

DEPA BILLABA sees terrible things in the Clone Wars and her troubled emotions lead her to the dark side.

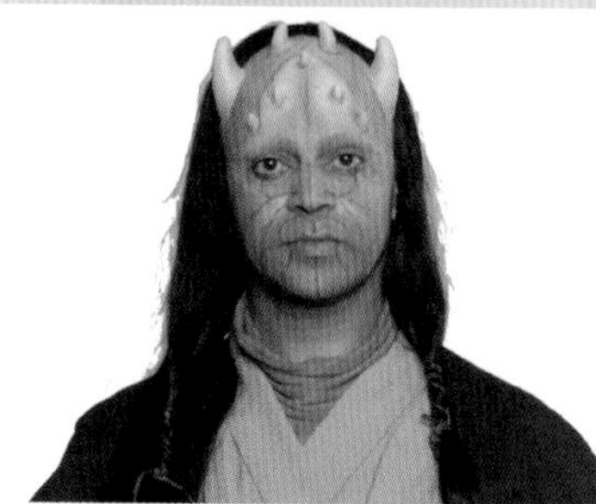

WILL OF STEEL

SPECIES: IRIDONIAN ZABRAK
HOMEWORLD: NAR SHADDAA

EETH KOTH works so hard at disciplining his mind that he can withstand great physical pain.

SUPER-SENSORY

SPECIES: TOGRUTA
HOMEWORLD: SHILI

SHAAK TI's hollow headtails allow her to sense her surroundings ultrasonically or duck blaster fire.

WAR WISDOM

SPECIES: THISSPIASIAN
HOMEWORLD: THISSPIAS

OPPO RANCISIS is a military mastermind and the Republic's secret weapon in the Clone Wars.

ATHLETIC JEDI

SPECIES: HUMAN
HOMEWORLD: KUAT

BULTAR SWAN is a fan of martial arts and this greatly influences the way she swings her lightsaber.

POWERFUL JEDI

SPECIES: UNKNOWN
HOMEWORLD: UNKNOWN

YADDLE has mastered Morichro—the ability to control others' body functions such as their breathing.

INJURED JEDI

SPECIES: LANNIK
HOMEWORLD: LANNIK

EVEN PIELL lost an eye in battle and he wears his scars as a reminder of past troubles.

LONER

SPECIES: IKTOTCHI
HOMEWORLD: IKTOTCH

SAESEE TIIN likes to spend time alone, meditating and honing his skill of foresight.

CUNNING JEDI

SPECIES: QUERMIAN
HOMEWORLD: QUERMIA

YARAEL POOF prefers not to use weapons—he uses his mastery of mind trickery against his enemies.

FAITHFUL JEDI

SPECIES: THOLOTHIAN
HOMEWORLD: CORUSCANT

ADI GALLIA is Stass Allie's cousin. She was inspired to be a Jedi as a child, when Even Piell saved her life.

FIERCE FIGHTER

SPECIES: IRIDONIAN ZABRAK
HOMEWORLD: CORUSCANT

AGEN KOLAR is no diplomat. Instead he prefers to influence people in battle, with his lightsaber.

OPEN-MINDED

SPECIES: ONGREE
HOMEWORLD: SKUSTELL

COLEMAN KCAJ's face shape allows him to see different angles. He can also see many sides to a problem.

LANGUAGE MASTER

SPECIES: VURK
HOMEWORLD: SEMBLA

COLEMAN TREBOR is a skilled communicator. He becomes the spokesperson for the Jedi Order.

BOOKWORM

SPECIES: HUMAN
HOMEWORLD: CORUSCANT

JOCASTA NU is a Consular Jedi. She is an academic, not a soldier, and looks after the Jedi Archives.

THE PATH TO THE...

POTENTIAL
As a child, Anakin shows great skill, but also much fear. The Jedi Council is unable to see his future and Anakin is too old, so it refuses to train him.

DEDICATION
Qui-Gon's dying wish is that Obi-Wan train Anakin. Although he is sometimes hot-headed and impatient, Anakin becomes a loyal Padawan.

ANGER
When his mother dies at the hands of Tusken Raiders, Anakin's anger consumes him. He destroys whole clan.

DEFIANCE
Anakin breaks the Jedi Code by marrying Padmé Amidala in secret. His love makes him so afraid of losing her that he is blinded to all else.

DARK SIDE

Anakin Skywalker is a great Jedi, but he struggles to control his feelings and greed. If Jedi do not keep their emotions in check, they are open to the temptations of the dark side. Darth Sidious covets Anakin as a Sith Apprentice so he plays with Anakin's emotions until they consume him and draw him over to the dark side.

POWER
During the Clone Wars, Anakin proves himself to be a brave Jedi hero. But he still wants more and feels that the Jedi are holding him back.

HATE
Anakin is goaded by Darth Sidious into killing Count Dooku. It is not the Jedi way to kill an unarmed prisoner, but Anakin gives in to his emotions.

GREED
Anakin is terrified Padmé will die. Darth Sidious claims he can save her, so Anakin greedily chooses the Sith over his fellow Jedi, and Mace dies.

EVIL
Anakin is given the Sith name Darth Vader. After fighting his old Master, Obi-Wan, Vader needs a metal suit to keep him alive. His journey to the dark side is complete.

WHAT HAPPENS WHEN A STUDENT TURNS ON HIS TEACHER?

THE BOND BETWEEN MASTER and Padawan is strong. From the moment Anakin turns to the dark side, a confrontation with his Master Obi-Wan Kenobi becomes inevitable. On Mustafar, Anakin rejects Obi-Wan's attempts to reason with him. Now serving a new master, a Sith master, Anakin isn't about to let any Jedi get in his way—even if that Jedi is one of his oldest friends.

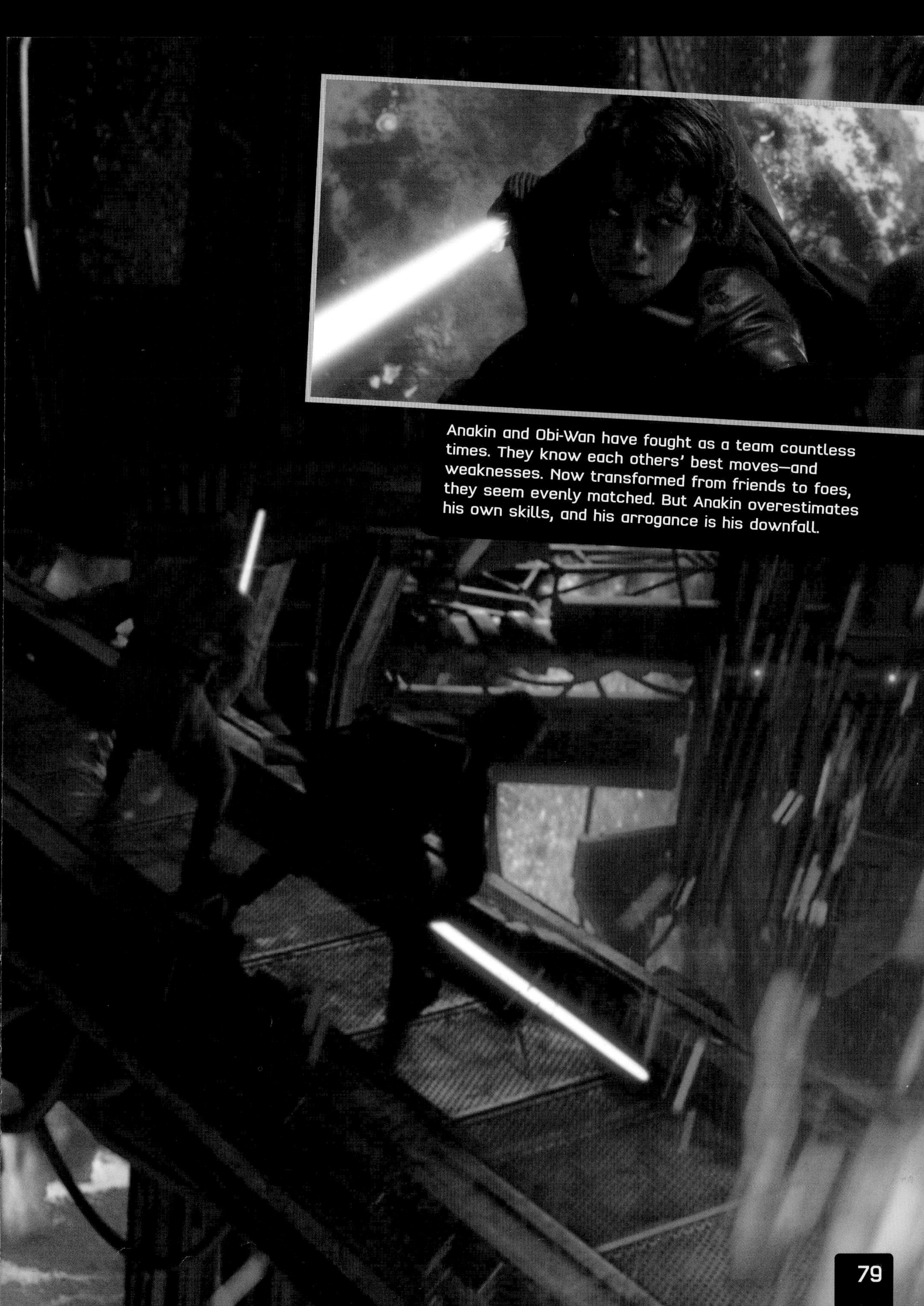

Anakin and Obi-Wan have fought as a team countless times. They know each others' best moves—and weaknesses. Now transformed from friends to foes, they seem evenly matched. But Anakin overestimates his own skills, and his arrogance is his downfall.

DARTH TYRANUS

Long ago Count Dooku rejected the Order that trained him as a Jedi. When Darth Maul is killed, Dooku becomes Darth Sidious's new Apprentice, Darth Tyranus.

DARTH MAUL

A Dathomirian trained in secret by Darth Sidious, Darth Maul is the first Sith to reveal himself for 1,000 years.

BEWARE THE SITH

FEAR...GREED...HATE...TYRANNY...these are the lifeblood of the Sith. The Sith are the oldest enemy of the Jedi. They, too, use the Force, but they have been seduced by the powers of its dark side. The Sith are driven by their greed for power and will not let anyone stand in their way—especially the Jedi.

DARTH VADER

Darth Vader is Sidious's final Apprentice. Vader is controlled by his Master and no longer bears any resemblance to the man he once was—Anakin Skywalker. His body is so damaged that he is dependent on a metal suit to keep him alive.

DARTH SIDIOUS

The Dark Lord of the Sith, Darth Sidious is a master of deception. For decades he fools everyone into thinking that he is the kind and peaceful Palpatine. In this guise, he rises to the position of Supreme Chancellor of the Republic and manipulates both sides in the Clone Wars. When the time comes to fulfill his master plan, he destroys the Republic and installs himself as Emperor of a new galactic order.

JEDI WISDOM

■ The Rule of Two states that there can be only two Sith at a time: one Master and one Apprentice. When Darth Sidious wants Anakin as an Apprentice, he manipulates him into killing Darth Tyranus.

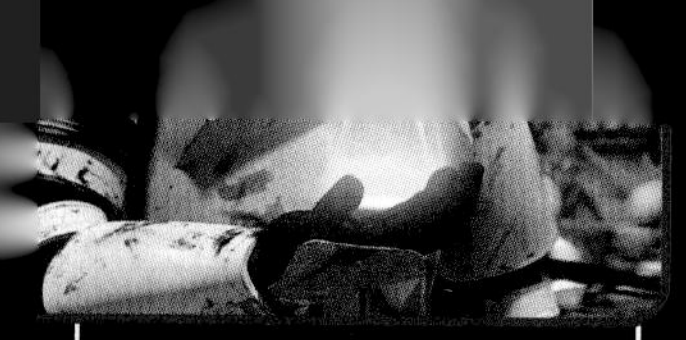

BREAKING NEWS: Rumors circulate that the clone troopers of the Republic Army have received executive orders from Chancellor Palpatine...

ORDER 66 is a secret military instruction created by Chancellor Palpatine to help him take over the galaxy. The Clone Army is programmed to follow the orders of the Chancellor, so when he gives Order 66, they have to act. The Clone Army turn on their former allies, the Jedi, with deadly consequences...

...UTAPAU: Commander Cody orders an AT-TE clone pilot to fire on Obi-Wan Kenobi...Jedi believed to have escaped...order issued to shoot on sight...

...FELUCIA: Commander Bly and the 327th Star Corps turn on Aayla Secura...Jedi confirmed dead...

...SALEUCAMI: Commander Neyo and CT-3423 fire on Stass Allie...death confirmed...

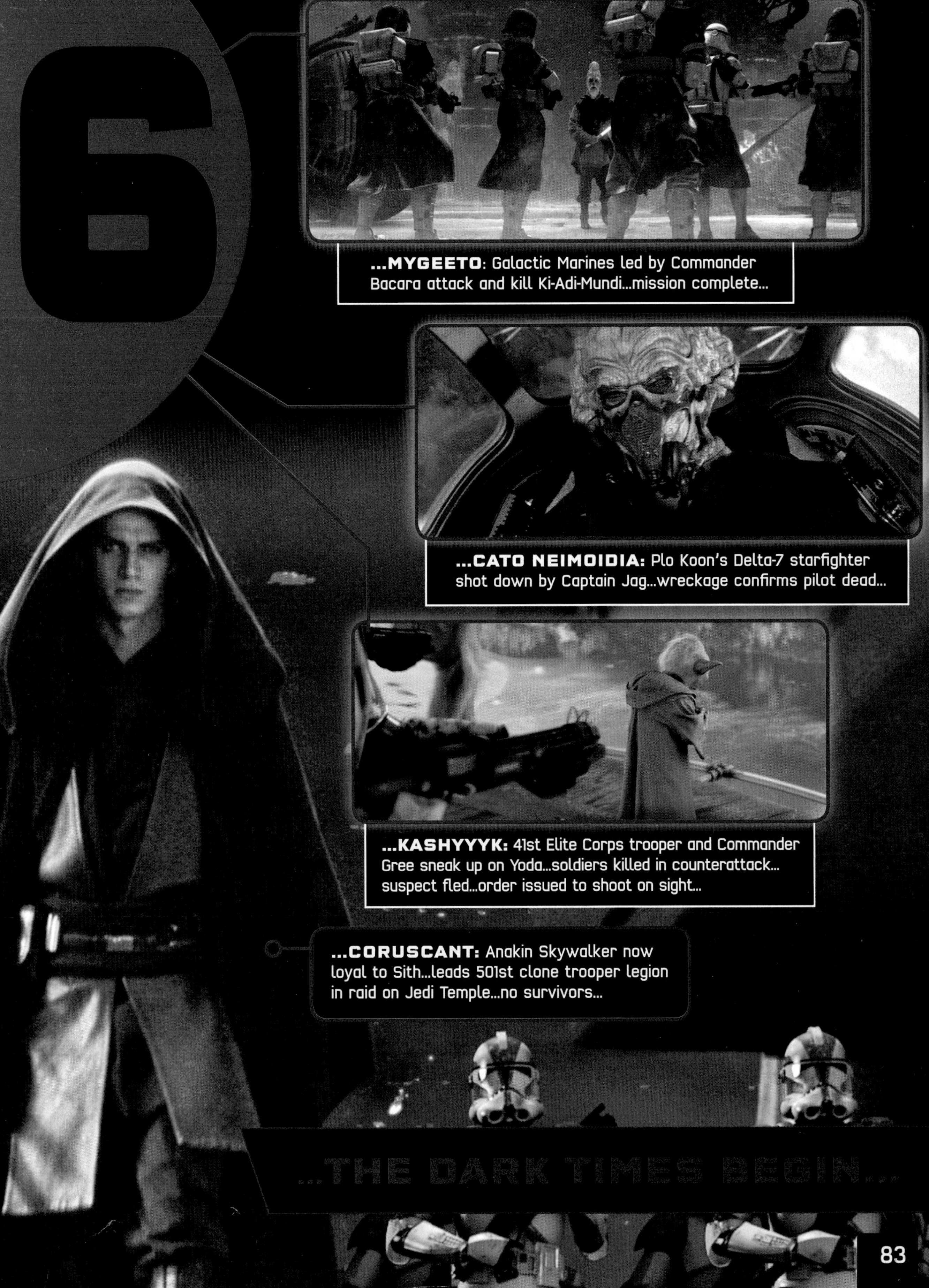
6
...MYGEETO: Galactic Marines led by Commander Bacara attack and kill Ki-Adi-Mundi...mission complete...
...CATO NEIMOIDIA: Plo Koon's Delta-7 starfighter shot down by Captain Jag...wreckage confirms pilot dead...
...KASHYYYK: 41st Elite Corps trooper and Commander Gree sneak up on Yoda...soldiers killed in counterattack... suspect fled...order issued to shoot on sight...
...CORUSCANT: Anakin Skywalker now loyal to Sith...leads 501st clone trooper legion in raid on Jedi Temple...no survivors...
...THE DARK TIMES BEGIN...

WHAT HAPPENS WHEN OLD ENEMIES MEET?

JEDI WISDOM

■ Some Jedi, like Obi-Wan, can make themselves one with the Force. This means that they can live on after death as part of the Force.

TWENTY YEARS HAVE passed since Darth Vader and Obi-Wan dueled on Mustafar. Aboard the Death Star, the former Jedi Master and his Padawan meet again. There is only hatred and revenge on Vader's mind, but Obi-Wan is serving a more important purpose. While the Rebels attempt to rescue Princess Leia, Obi-Wan engages Vader in a duel.

Although Obi-Wan is still a match for Darth Vader, he allows himself to be killed in the duel, giving Luke and the Rebels precious time to escape. Unlike Vader, who tries to control death, Obi-Wan is willing to submit to it: He passes over to the non-physical to show Luke that his spirit can continue beyond death.

SEPARATED AT BIRTH
When Luke sets off to rescue a princess, he finds more than he bargained for: a twin sister. He is fiercely protective of his sister, Leia, and does everything he can to keep her safe.

Luke always sees the good in people, even someone as cruel as Darth Vader. He never gives up hope that his father will change.

Luke SKYWALKER

Luke is an adventure-seeking boy from Tatooine who brings new hope to the Rebel Alliance and the few remaining Jedi. He comes to Jedi training late in life, but the Force is strong with him and he is guided by a wiser Obi-Wan and Yoda. Luke faces a daunting task: to defeat Darth Vader and the Emperor.

JEDI STATS

SPECIES: HUMAN
HOMEWORLD: BORN ON POLIS MASSA; RAISED ON TATOOINE
BIRTHDATE: 19 BBY
HEIGHT: 1.72 M (5 FT 8 IN)
RANK: JEDI MASTER
TRAINED BY: OBI-WAN & YODA
WEAPON: BLUE & LATER A GREEN-BLADED LIGHTSABER
PREFERRED COMBAT STYLE: FORM V (SHIEN/DJEM SO)
TRADEMARK: LOYALTY

EXCEPTIONAL CONNECTION WITH THE FORCE

HIS FATHER'S SON?

Luke's father is Anakin Skywalker. Like him, Luke is a good pilot and has a knack for knowing how to fix things, and he can also be impatient and reckless. However, Luke differs from his father in one key way: Despite the Emperor's best efforts, Luke refuses to submit to the dark side.

LIGHTSABER ONCE BELONGED TO ANAKIN

FAITHFUL FRIEND

Luke shows great loyalty to his friends, even the droids. To Luke, astromech droid R2-D2 is far more than just a robot, and he wouldn't swap him for the world.

Wampas are deadly ice creatures who aren't fussy about what or whom they eat. A human wouldn't normally stand a chance against these mighty beasts, but Luke has a special weapon—the Force.

HOW CAN YOU ESCAPE FROM A FIERCE WAMPA?

Luke closes his eyes and concentrates hard—just like Obi-Wan taught him. After a few moments, the lightsaber zips through the air, right into Luke's hand! He uses it to cut himself down and escape the wampa.

PATROLLING THE FREEZING plains of Hoth, Luke Skywalker is attacked by a wampa ice monster. The next thing he knows, he's suspended by his ankles in an icy cave. Luke knows he's in trouble. If only he could reach his lightsaber, lying just a few feet away...

HOW CAN THE LIGHT SIDE OF THE FORCE DEFEAT THE DARK SIDE?

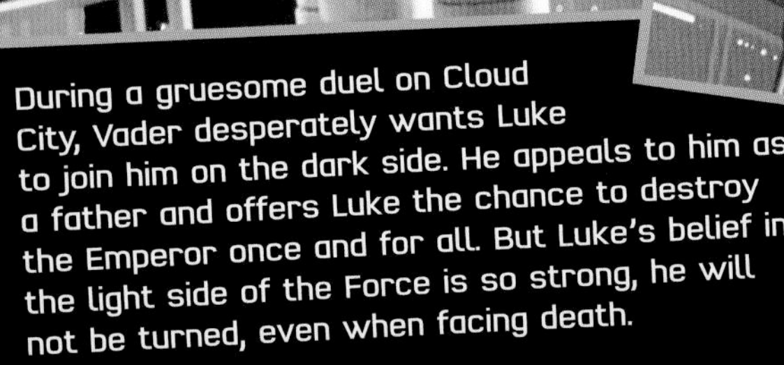

During a gruesome duel on Cloud City, Vader desperately wants Luke to join him on the dark side. He appeals to him as a father and offers Luke the chance to destroy the Emperor once and for all. But Luke's belief in the light side of the Force is so strong, he will not be turned, even when facing death.

Luke resists the dark side again during another duel with his father on the second Death Star. Luke's extreme dedication to the light side shames his father, and when the Emperor attempts to kill Luke, Vader hears Luke's pleas and rescues his son. As he dies, Vader finally finds peace in the light side of the Force.

THE AGE-OLD battle between Jedi and Sith, between the light and dark sides of the Force, has always hinged on temptation. Sith Lords often recruit Jedi with promises of incredible power. However, sometimes the desire for honor and justice can be powerful, too.

GLOSSARY

ASTROMECH DROID
■ A utility robot that repairs and helps navigate starships.

BATTLE DROID
■ A Separatist robot designed for combat.

BATTLE OF GEONOSIS
■ Conflict in 22 BBY where the Republic Clone Army attacks the Separatists' battle droid army on the planet Geonosis, marking the start of the Clone Wars.

BATTLE OF NABOO
■ Conflict in 32 BBY where the Trade Federation invades the planet Naboo with their battle droid army.

BLOCKADE
■ A political strategy that prevents food and resources from reaching a specific destination.

BOUNTY HUNTER
■ Someone who tracks down, captures, or kills wanted people in exchange for money.

BUREAUCRATIC
■ Consisting of lots of time-consuming office work.

BUZZ DROIDS
■ Small droids that latch onto and sabotage enemy spacecraft; often used by Separatist forces in space battles.

CEREAN
■ A species from the planet Cerea; Cereans are similar to humans but have tall heads to house their double brains.

CHANCELLOR
■ The title given to the head of the Galactic Senate and Republic.

CHOSEN ONE
■ The subject of an ancient prophecy referring to an individual who will restore balance to the Force and to the universe.

CLONE ARMY
■ An army of genetically identical soldiers, all trained to be perfect warriors. They fight for the Republic.

CLONE WARS
■ A series of galaxy-wide battles fought between the Republic's Clone Army and the droid army of the Confederacy of Independent Systems, which took place between 22–19 BBY.

CORUSCANT
■ The capital of the Republic. This planet is home to the Senate Building, the Jedi Temple, and the Jedi Council.

CYBORG
■ A being that is partly a living organism and partly a robot.

DARK SIDE
■ The evil side of the Force that feeds off negative emotions and offers raw power to those who study it.

DEMOCRACY
■ A system of government where all senior politicians are elected by the population.

DROIDEKA
■ A destroyer droid used in battle by the Separatists.

EMPEROR
■ Ruler of the Empire.

EMPIRE
■ A tyrannical power that rules the galaxy from 19 BBY to 4 ABY under the leadership of the Emperor, who is a Sith Lord.

FORCE
■ The energy that flows through all living things, which can used for either good or evil.

FORCE LIGHTNING
■ Deadly rays of blue energy that can be used as a weapon by someone who has embraced the dark side of the Force.

GRAND MASTER
■ The leader of the Jedi High Council.

GUNGANS
■ An amphibious species from the planet Naboo.

JEDI
■ A member of the Jedi Order who studies the light side of the Force.

JEDI ARCHIVES
■ The large collection of research and knowledge about the history of the Jedi Order; housed in the Jedi Temple.

JEDI CODE
■ The set of rules that establishes the behavior and lifestyle of members of the Jedi Order.

JEDI HIGH COUNCIL
■ The 12 senior, respected members of the Jedi Order who meet to make important decisions and give advice.

JEDI KNIGHT
■ A member of the Jedi Order who has studied as a Padawan under a Jedi Master and who has passed the Jedi Trials.

JEDI MASTER
■ A rank for Jedi Knights who have performed an exceptional deed or have trained a Jedi Knight.

JEDI ORDER
■ An ancient organization that promotes peace and justice throughout the galaxy.

JEDI PURGE
■ The attempt by Chancellor Palpatine in 19 BBY to annihilate the entire Jedi Order.

JEDI TEMPLE
■ The headquarters of the Jedi Order, located on the planet Coruscant.

LIGHTSABER
■ A weapon with a blade of pure energy that is used by Jedi and Sith warriors.

LIVING FORCE
■ The view that the Force is present in all living things. Living by this view means relying on instincts, being aware of the people around you, and living in the moment.

MENTOR
■ A wise teacher or advisor who gives guidance.

NABOO
■ A beautiful planet near the border of the Outer Rim Territories.

ORDER 66
■ An order given by Chancellor Palpatine that began the Jedi Purge. Every clone trooper in the Clone Army was ordered to kill all members of the Jedi Order.

PADAWAN
■ A Youngling who is chosen to serve an apprenticeship with a Jedi Master.

PODRACING
■ A popular sport, especially on the planet Tatooine, in which competitors race against each other in high-powered Podracers.

REBEL ALLIANCE
■ The organization that resists and fights against the Empire.

REPUBLIC
■ The democratic government of the galaxy, under leadership of an elected Chancellor.

SENATE
■ Government of the Republic, with representatives from all parts of the galaxy.

SENATOR
■ A person who represents their planet, sector, or system in the Senate.

SEPARATISTS
■ An alliance against the Republic. Also known also the Confederacy of Independent Systems.

SITH
■ An ancient sect of Force-sensitives who study the dark side to gain control and succeed in their greedy plans.

TRADE FEDERATION
■ A bureaucratic organization that controls much of the trade and commerce in the galaxy.

TUSKEN RAIDERS
■ Fearsome savages who live in the desert wastelands of the planet Tatooine; also known as Sand People.

TWI'LEK
■ A species from the planet Ryloth. Twi'leks have colorful skin and a pair of tentacles (lekku) that grow from their heads.

YOUNGLING
■ A Force-sensitive child who joins the Jedi Order to be trained in the Jedi arts.

ZABRAK
■ A species native to the planet Iridonia. Zabraks have small horns on the top of their heads.

INDEX

Characters are listed under their most frequently used common name, for example Luke Skywalker is found under "L" and "Count Dooku" is under "C."

Main entries are in bold.

A

B

C

D

LONDON, NEW YORK, MELBOURNE,
MUNICH, AND DELHI

For Dorling Kindersley
Editor Shari Last
Senior Editor Elizabeth Dowsett
Designer Toby Truphet
Senior Designer Lynne Moulding
Additional design by Owen Bennett, Nathan Martin,
Rob Perry, Rhys Thomas
Managing Art Editor Ron Stobbart
Publishing Manager Catherine Saunders
Art Director Lisa Lanzarini
Associate Publisher Simon Beecroft
Category Publisher Alex Allan
Production Editor Siu Yin Chan
Production Controller Nick Seston

For Lucasfilm
Executive Editor J. W. Rinzler
Art Director Troy Alders
Keeper of the Holocron Leland Chee
Director of Publishing Carol Roeder

First published in the United States in 2011
by DK Publishing
375 Hudson Street, New York, New York 10014

11 12 13 14 15 10 9 8 7 6 5 4 3 2 1
178200—12/10

A catalog record for this book is
available from the Library of Congress.

ISBN: 978-0-7566-7197-6

Color reproduction by Media Development Printing Ltd
Printed and bound in Singapore by Star Standard

The publisher would like to thank Chris Trevas and Chris Reiff for their artwork on pages 42–43 and Julia March and Victoria Taylor for their editorial work.

Discover more at
www.dk.com
www.starwars.com